D0638840

AMAZING GRACE

AMAZING GRACE

By

L. E. BARTON, M.A., D.D.

THE CHRISTOPHER PUBLISHING HOUSE
BOSTON, U.S.A.

CONTENTS

INTRODUCTION

Dr. L. E. Barton, an ordained minister for well over fifty years, sets a good example for the minister by not letting his years deter him from working. These sermons evince a goodly amount of research in the Greek New Testament and in wide reading.

Besides pastorates in his native state, Arkansas, he has wrought in this capacity in Virginia, Georgia, Mississippi, and Alabama. He has served in various positions among Southern Baptists, including several important committees of the Southern Baptist Convention. He was elected as vice president of the Convention in 1927, and official Parliamentarian in 1947 and 1948. Besides editorial experience, he has written several books.

He received his M.A. degree from Union University, Jackson, Tennessee, which school bestowed on him the D.D. degree in 1911. Besides, he did work at the Southern Baptist Theological Seminary in Louisville, Kentucky. For many years he has appeared in Who's Who in America.

These sermons show how a knowledge of the Greek New Testament can be turned into practical blessing in preaching. The best preaching is that which comes bathed in a serious historical and grammatical exegesis of the text. It is a false scholarship of our day that thinks to preach without an exegetical background. Such study is not all, but it is a good beginning in the right direction.

Expository preaching is not as common as one could wish. This series of messages shows how warmhearted and practical expository preaching can be. Expository preaching is that type of sermon which sets forth in a practical way the meaning of the Bible. It begins with exegesis, the work in the study, and becomes exposition when the presentation of the meaning of the text looks toward an audience. Dr. Barton never forgets his listener.

Evangelical emphasis lies at the heart of these expository discussions. The doctrines of grace are set forth with warm devotion and simple faith in the word of God as the trustworthy revelation evangelicals have all along believed it to be. No one will find here any catering to human merit and human effort for salvation. Salvation is shown to be a matter of the unmerited favor of God bestowed on hell-deserving sinners, from its inception in the heart of God to its consummation in the believer's glorification. Due emphasis is given to the responsibility of the sinner to repent and believe the glorious gospel.

This stress on divine grace prepares the way for balanced emphasis on the fruition of grace in the believer's consecration to daily application of the gospel in all relations of life. The social application of the gospel must never forget the source of salvation in the all-embracing grace of God in Christ Jesus. Clean living is the natural fruit of preaching the atoning blood of Jesus our Lord as the only ground of justification of the sinner before a righteous God.

Church relations and duties are emphasized in a clear presentation of the church question. The writer of these sermons has given a sane exposition of the knotty problems of the nature of the New Testament church in its manifestation now and in its anticipated consummation later.

One word more will finish the writer's characterization of these sermons which warmed his heart greatly. They

are Christo-centric. Too much of modern life is anthro-
po-centric. Man is important, but our lives and our
preaching must be Christo-centric, all centered in the
Lord Jesus. Without Him, we are nothing in our lack
of saving merit; saved by Him and called into His service, we are still nothing except as the indwelling Christ
lives out through us His risen and triumphant life. His
evangelistic, missionary, and soul-winning purpose in
the dealings of grace with and in and through us must
ever look toward the greater glory of Christ Jesus our
Lord while the ages unfold.

I write these words with the confidence that these
homilies wait to do for your soul what they did for mine.

—*Roy Beaman*

Study,
New Orleans Baptist Seminary

PREFACE

Smith's history of Greece says (p. 117), "The earliest
Greek Colonies were those founded on the western shores
of Asia Minor. The Aeolic cities covered the northern
part of this coast; the Ionians occupied the center and
the Dorians the southern part." Ephesus is said to have
been an Ionian City. Grote's Greece, a work of twelve
volumes, accredits the founding of Ephesus to Androk-
lus. One authority says that the settlers were Hellenic,
chiefly Ionians, and Orientals. But Pausanias tells of
strangers who lived there before the Ionians came. Some
modern scholars believe that these were of the warring
Hittites whom Joshua encountered in the conquest of
Palestine. The population of Ephesus in Paul's time included, doubtless, many Asiatics.

The city stood at the crossroads of trade routes and
converged on the communication line between the em-
poria of the East and metropolitan Rome on the West.
Four rivers, with fertile valleys, penetrated Asia Minor.
Miletus, where Paul met the Ephesian elders, was on
the Meander. Pergamus was on the Caicus, Smyrna on
the Hermus, and Ephesus was situated not far from
the mouth of the Cayster. The latter was the chief city
of that productive area. It was located on the left bank
of that river near its mouth which made Ephesus a seaport
as long as the channel was kept clear. Speaking of the
valley of the Cayster river Conybeare and Howson, *Life
and Epistles of Paul, says*: "Here in a situation pre-
eminent among the excellent positions which the Ionians
chose for their cities Ephesus was built on some hills

13

near the sea—In the time of St. Paul it was the greatest
city of Asia Minor, as well as the metropolis of the province of Asia." David Smith, in *The Life and Letters of
St. Paul*, says (p. 235), "Situated close to the mouth of
the river Cayster, she (Ephesus) was a busy seaport with
extensive docks despite the troublesome accumulation
of alluvial deposit." *Adam's Biblical Backgrounds* (p.
453), gives the distance of Ephesus from the sea as three
miles.

"The commercial supremacy of Miletus under Greek
sovereignty passed to Ephesus under Roman Rule. The
overthrow of Smyrna by the Lydians about 525 B.C.
and of Miletus by the Persians B.C. 494 contributed to
the importance and ascendancy of Ephesus." Thus, in
the Roman Empire Ephesus ranked with Antioch and
Alexandria as one of the three great cities of the Levant.

Ephesus was a "free city" with an assembly and a council, and a proconsul, or Governor; in other words, a
"colony," or a little Rome that managed its own affairs
with only general supervision from Rome. The famous
Temple of Diana (Latin) or Artemis (Greek) was located here with its revered statue, which, tradition said,
fell from heaven.

The temple erected to Diana was one of the seven
wonders of the world at that time. Pliny (Natural History) says that it was 425 by 220 feet in dimensions.
Another authority however gives the size as 343 by 164
feet, with 127 columns 60 feet high, the whole structure being of shining marble. This shrine, thought to
have been 220 years in the building, contained the sacred
statue, behind which was the treasury, the bank of Asia.
The Temple was destroyed by the Goths in A.D. 262.

The city exists today only as a wretched Turkish
village under the name Ayasaluk. Besides the world's

wonder temple, Ephesus could boast of the largest and most splendid theatre of the ancient Greek world, which accommodated fifty thousand spectators of the games and gladiatorial contests.

North of this was a stadium where racing and fights of wild beasts were conducted. The chief glory of Ephesus was her title "neokoros" "temple keeper," literally, "temple sweeper." The word is translated "worshipper" by the King James version (Acts 19:35), and "temple keeper" by the Revised Version. Inscriptions of the second, and coins of the third, century have been cited by Prof. Ramsay which bear witness to the fact stated in Acts 19:35 that Ephesus had the title of "Warden of the Temple of Diana."

The names of Paul and Timothy and Priscilla (more correctly Prisca) and Acquila are associated in Scripture with Ephesus; and Eusebius, who wrote a church history in the third century, tells us that the apostle John made his residence there in his later life. Eusebius gives numerous interesting incidents which occurred during John's stay there.

When Paul went out on his second missionary tour, he was forbidden of the Spirit to preach the word in Asia (Acts 16:6) in which province Ephesus was situated; but at the close of that journey on his return from Greece to Syria he visited Ephesus and "reasoned with the Jews in the synagogues" (Acts 18:19-21). He had to press on to Jerusalem to the feast but left Prisca and Acquila at Ephesus (Acts 18:18-21). It seems therefore that the church of Ephesus grew out of Paul's first visit and the follow-up work of Prisca and her noble husband.

Some students, among them so able a scholar as De-Wette, "who with an almost incredible lack of insight, have considered this book (Ephesians) an insipid produc-

tion or a tedious and unskillful composition" (Ex. G.T.).
Such monstrous announcements belong to the failures
of inept and hostile criticism. Nearly all scholars of all
schools of thought have regarded Ephesians as one of
the most profound and sublime of New Testament books.
One heard Henry G. Weston, President of Crozier Seminary, say that it is the greatest writing ever penned by
mortal man. A. T. Robertson quotes Stalker to the same
effect.

What was the destination of this epistle? Was it written specifically to the church at Ephesus, or was it an
encyclical letter for all the churches in the Ephesian
area, that is, a general letter to the churches in the Roman
province of Asia? The traditional view said: "To Ephesus specifically." Studies in modern times have convinced
many able interpreters, most interpreters perhaps, that
it is an encyclical, or circular letter sent to all the churches
in that area; and was to be read in the churches (and a
copy to be made and kept) and then sent on to the next
church until all had read and copied it.

That is the way this writer sees it, and yet the point
is not paramount, because, whatever its destination, the
letter is unquestionably divine truth, which brings its
message to all the churches of that day and of our day.
(See first Chapter for fuller discussion).

The eternal purpose of God concerning the salvation
of his people is expressed in verse four, chapter one—
"According as He chose us in Him before the foundation of the world that we should be holy and without
blame before Him." The effective, practical application
of that purpose is expressed in verse seven of the same
chapter—"In whom we have redemption through His
blood, the forgiveness of sins according to the riches of
his grace." This perfected work in believers is set forth

in chapter two, verse eight.—"For by grace have ye been saved through faith and that not of yourselves, it is the gift of GOD, not of works, that no man should glory." The "mystery" of which he speaks in chapter three had been hidden from the ages in God. This was that the Gentiles are fellow-heirs and fellow-members of the body and fellow-partakers of the promise in Christ Jesus through the gospel, which is to be preached to all the world in order that now there might be made known to the rulerships and the powers in the heavenly places through the church the manifold wisdom of God, according to the purpose of the ages which He made in Christ Jesus our Lord in whom we have boldness and access in confidence through faith in him (See Chap. 3:2-12). The glory of God in the church and in Christ Jesus forever, 3:21. These are the basis of the great things Paul tells us in Ephesians.

The purpose of this book is to give through expository sermons an exposition of Ephesians in such a method as to be helpful both to the common reader and to students.

The most of the Scripture quotations are from the American Standard Version, although at times the author has given his own rendering of the Greek text, as he has studied the passages with the aid of such works as the *Expositor's Greek Testament*, Robertson's *Word Pictures*, Expository notes of the *Pulpit Commentary*, Olshausen's *Commentaries*, Maclaren's *Expositions*, with a careful and constant examination of the words in the *Lexicon*.

It is a major undertaking to write a book on Ephesians. Perhaps the author has some qualification for the task in his joy in Ephesians, and it may be that forty years of study of the book and much preaching from it, and teaching it many times in churches and Bible Conferences will be some reason, if not a defense, for his asking a hearing on so difficult a subject. The present form of the text is the result of three writings of the ms. with a good deal of special labor within the last six or seven years. If he has been able to help the average reader, and his fellow preachers of the Word to a deeper and more correct understanding of Paul's greatest of all interpretations of the grace of God and the glory of God in the salvation of His people, then he will be happy, and grateful for the privilege.

Effort has been made to give proper credit in the text for quotations. But it has not been thought necessary or wise to "footnote" every well known quotation.

The author expresses profound gratitude to a beloved nephew, Eugene C. Barton, for his encouragement and financial aid in the publication of this volume by an advance order, for five hundred copies to be given to theological students.

Appreciation is due Dr. R. G. Lee, Dr. W. A. Criswell, Dr. C. G. Campbell, and Dr. A. G. Moseley who have read the MS and made helpful suggestions. The author is grateful indeed to Dr. Roy Beaman, who, with skill and competency, read the ms. and made valuable criticisms. Moreover his gracious introduction increases my debt of abiding gratitude.

Ex. G. T. means Expositor's Greek Testament.

Ex. B. is The Expositor's Bible.

Maclaren refers to Alexander Maclaren's Expositions. Robertson, without initials, refers to A. T. Robertson in his Word Pictures. Others quoted are spelled out in the text.

Amazing Grace

I

GRACE AND PEACE

"Paul, an apostle of Christ Jesus through the will of God to the saints that are at Ephesus and the faithful in Christ Jesus; grace to you and peace from God our Father and from our Lord Jesus Christ" (Ephesians 1:1, 2).

Strolling through Westminster Abbey one day in 1934, one came upon a large dark marble slab in the floor on which was engraved in large letters the name "Livingstone." Feeling richly rewarded for the tour of research through the ancient, historic pile one reverted to the Scotsman's parents, and boyhood, and school days and to his leave-taking when his father walked the seven miles with him from Blantyre to Glasgow to bid him goodbye as the young missionary left home to begin his career. His labors, his studies and endless explorations in Africa, and his love for the natives and their devotion to him came to mind. Moreover the elements of drama and tragedy in his life were not forgotten. When he was lost to the world somewhere in the dark, and unknown, continent and a New York paper sent Henry M. Stanley at any cost to find him, millions waited with bated breath

19

for news of the great missionary. When taps were sounded and he answered the last roll call on his knees at the side of his rude bed, after he had scribbled in the dim light on a piece of scrap paper: "May heaven's blessings come down on every one whether Christian, Jew or Mohammedan, who will help to heal this open sore of the world, the African slave trade," his body was borne by the natives to the coast, where it was put on a ship to go back to London to sleep in Westminster until the Lord shall raise and clothe it with immortality.

One thinks we may paraphrase Paul's first statement without violence to the truth: "Livingstone an apostle of Christ Jesus through the will of God to the lost of Africa."

There are striking parallels between Paul and Livingstone. Both were men of good poise, sound judgment, great mentality, fine training, complete surrender to God, perfect obsession with their life purpose. They both counted all things as refuse for the excellence of Christ. They both labored to their utmost ability and endured all things for the elect's sake. They were pioneers, building on no other man's foundation, who were continually carving out the material for building the kingdom of God in lands where Christ had been hitherto unknown. In other words they were true apostles.

"Apostle" means one sent away on a mission. He is a man under authority, a man who bears a message of supreme importance from the dignitary who has sent him forth. He may be an ambassador carrying the mandate of a king, or an emissary who is hastening with a message of clemency, or pardon, to set at liberty one who is accused of crime, or a courier carrying tidings or orders in war. He may be one sent by a father with a message of love to his son. He is one who bears the message of his master and not his own. He must guard the safety and integrity of the message with his own life if necessary. The message is the main thing. It must be delivered at any cost. Life or death is at the other end of the line waiting for the message to arrive and determine which it shall be. A pardon from Governor Vardaman of Mississippi for a Negro in Issaquena County reached the sheriff five minutes after the Negro was executed—the tragedy of a late message.

Paul goes further in his statement. He is an apostle through the will of God. He is motivated by divine purpose and energized by supreme power. Just here lies the difference between the strength and weakness of a life. Ahimaaz ran without a message, hence had nothing to say when he arrived.

The sender of this message is Christ Jesus, the risen and reigning Lord. The messenger is the apostle who belongs to Him and is commissioned by Him. The operating authority and dynamic of the message is God's supreme will. The objective is the saints, all the faithful in Christ Jesus. For dignity, majesty, urgency, imperious authority, and implementation of power what could rival this mission of an apostle of Christ Jesus through the will of God?

Paul says that he is an apostle "to the saints who are also faithful in Christ Jesus." That seems to be the correct text, instead of the reading of the common version: "To the saints who are in Ephesus and to the faithful in Christ Jesus." The form of the reading turns, largely though not alone, on whether the words "In Ephesus" are genuine.

There are arguments on both sides more or less cogent, but one believes that the preponderating evidence re-

quires that "in Ephesus" must be omitted. The two
oldest and best manuscripts do not have these words.
Then, Origen (c185-c254) the most famous Christian
writer and teacher of the third century, shows plainly
from his translation of the sentence that the words "in
Ephesus" were not in the manuscript which was before
him. Marcion, who lived in the second century, calls
Ephesians the epistle to the Laodiceans. Marcion was
a Gnostic heretic whom the Christians rejected, but that
fact would not invalidate his testimony as to the identi-
fication of this epistle. If we connect his statements
with Colossians 4:16, which speaks of "the letter from
Laodicea" we shall probably have the explanation: that
is, that the Laodicean letter was this one on its rounds.
Dr. Robertson says: "After writing the stirring Epistle
to the Colossians Paul dictated this so-called Epistle to
the Ephesians as a general or circular letter for the
churches in Asia, (Roman Province). Perhaps the original
copy had no name in 1:1 as seen in Aleph and B and
Origen, but only a blank space. Marcion was familiar
with the copy in Laodicea. Basil in the fourth century
mentions some MSS. with no name in the address. Most
MSS. were copies from the one in Ephesus and so it
came to be called the Epistle to the Ephesians. The general nature of the letter explains also the absence of
names in it, though Paul lived three years in Ephesus." A
translation which satisfies the grammar perfectly, with
"in Ephesus" omitted, is: "To the saints who are also
faithful in Christ Jesus." That is also more harmonious
with the meaning of the passage. "To the saints who are
in Ephesus and to the faithful in Christ Jesus" seems to
differentiate between the saints in Ephesus and some
other class. In fact, if it had been addressed "to the saints
who are in Ephesus" it would have been superfluous to

add: "and to the faithful in Christ Jesus," unless it had added "and to *all* the saints who are faithful in Christ Jesus."

Now, what is the meaning of "faithful in Christ Jesus"? Some have suggested: "To the saints who have faith in Christ Jesus." That is permissible so far as the grammar is concerned, but it is wholly superfluous, and almost ridiculous to suggest that saints should have faith in Christ. It has been taken by others to designate a class, "believers in Christ." Some think it means "trustworthy or loyal to Christ." But in that case we should not have had the preposition "in." Perhaps it's better to take it as a Locative Case—they are in Christ, hence they stand faithful, loyal and true. They are faithful by virtue of their union with him—the one essential and power that produces holy character and behavior.

After orienting and identifying himself, and presenting his divine credentials, Paul expressed the content of his message, "Grace to you and peace from God our Father and from the Lord Jesus Christ."

Study of the word grace will be rewarding to any who make such investigation. The Lexicon defines the Greek word for grace (*charis*) as follows:

1. "Properly that which affords joy, pleasure, delight, sweetness, charm, loveliness"
2. "Good will, loving kindness, favor."

Another definition is "thanks, recompense, reward." Again "*charis*" is used of "the kindness of a master toward his inferiors or servants, and especially of God toward men. It also contains the idea of kindness which bestows upon one what he has not deserved."

Then comes the New Testament sense of this great word. "Charis (grace) is used of the merciful kindness by which God, exerting his holy influence upon souls, turns them to Christ, keeps, strengthens, increases them in Christian faith, knowledge, affection, and kindles them to the exercise of Christian virtues." So this great word took on this larger content with New Testament writers, especially with Paul. Paul never used the Old Testament phrase or idea of "finding" grace and favor with the Lord." We do not find grace, it finds us. It is "God giving to men, acting upon men, moving in the life of His people. The grace of God or of His Son deals with men in their mortal weakness and estrangement, reconciling them to Him. All is of grace in the religious life. Hence Paul sees grace as at once a release and a challenge, a gift and a demand, a free pardon that strips men of self-esteem and also a summons that brings them to their feet with the glow of expectation," (James Moffatt in *Grace in the New Testament*).

The Greek word for grace (*charis*) brought before the Greek mind the beauty of form, the accomplishments of conduct, the elegance of diction or speech, the brilliance and power of oratory, the stateliness of palaces, the charm of feminine character, the perfection of literary style. Occasionally in Greek literature it reached up into a higher realm and expressed the idea of kindness to others, even forgiveness to a friend or foe. This higher sense of the word, enlivened and glorified by the love and mercy of God in forgiving his enemies through the sacrificial death of Christ Jesus, is the content that Paul and other New Testament writers pour into this word. They do not discount or despise beauty, elegance, charm, and loveliness, all of which are by-products in the hearts of men, of the mercy and love and forgiveness of God, but they hold grace to that one great conception of God's seeking, redeeming, saving, and sanctifying men because of His eternal benevolence and prevenient

love. Grace therefore is the active, aggressive, militant
(if you will) nature of God, combining all his mercy,
love and compassion and going on an endless quest for
lost and ruined men. It is as diligent and determined as
a mother seeking her lost child. "As one whom his
mother comforts so will I comfort thee." The Sunday
paper of July 1, 1953, showed the picture of a most
handsome and husky soldier hovering tenderly over his
sick mother. He had flown from Korea to the States
so that his mother who was going blind could look on
his face once more before darkness settled forever on
her sight. She said: "Now that I have got a last look
at his happy face I can live and die happy."

Yes, long before you ever sought God He was seeking you.

"I sought the Lord, but afterwards I knew
He moved my soul to it who sought for me;
It was not I that found, O Savior true,
Nay, I was found of Thee.

Thou didst stretch forth Thine hand
And mine enfold;
I walked and sank not on the storm-vexed sea,
But not so much that I on Thee had hold,
As by Thy hold on me.

Now I walk, I love, but ah the whole of love
Is but my answer, Lord to Thee;
Lord, Thou wast long time beforehand with my soul,
Always Thou lovedst me."

"No one can tell all that is wrapped up in grace. It is
as gentle as the morning breeze, and mighty as the ocean
tide. It suggests spontaneous favor—the bestowal of
rich benefits on one who has no right to receive them.

Grace is energy making the weak strong, wealth making the poor rich, life making the dead live. It is the Christian's alphabet out of which he writes his songs, upon which he builds his hopes, and from which he draws his comforts. It is the foundation of his feet, the canopy for his head, the music of his soul. No wonder the hymn writer sang:

> "Marvelous grace of our loving Lord,
> Grace that exceeds our sin and our guilt,
> Yonder on Calvary's mount outpoured
> There where the blood of the Lamb was spilt."
> —Ralph E. Rhyne.

Grace is mercy dying for rebels. Grace produces and plummets the depths of Calvary. Grace brings life and immortality to light through the resurrection. "Grace is love out-loving love," said Dr. Philips in his Baptist World Alliance sermon at Philadelphia. Paul would not say less and he could not say more.

Notice the sequence here, not "peace and grace" but "grace and peace." You will never find the apostle's order changed. The soul that will not accept grace can never have peace. A world, a nation that knows not grace is not only a stranger to peace but a feudist, and a warmonger. A church that is not founded and fortified in grace will be frustrated by faction and defeated by divisions. But this is not a political or national peace, devoutly as we should strive for that. It is the peace of the Spirit that passeth understanding.

Preachers are shouting, "Be good, be good" to millions who have never passed through the valley of repentance and confession of sin into the redemption which is in Christ. You had as well admonish a thistle to bear

figs or a thorn bush to be clothed with grapes as to expect an unregenerate, unforgiven man to bear the spiritual
fruits of a life in Christ. Man has no power to redeem
himself, neither any power to bring forth the fruits of
righteousness except as Christ abides within him and the
Spirit of God sanctifies him through the word of truth.
It is "the grace of God that bringeth salvation which has
appeared to all men" that regenerates the soul through
the Holy Spirit; that breaks the chains of sin; that gives
a daily sense of sin and of the need for the transforming
of the whole life into the image of Christ. If we could
be done with the nervous, fidgety effort to bear fruit
apart from Christ, and give the grace of God full sway
and sweep in our spirit the fruit would come in its season
as the result of spiritual cause and effect.

Nothing is more helpless and tragic than the uncon-
trolled, unsanctified talents of a human life. It is like
a big ship that has lost its way, or has been driven ashore
and now cannot navigate the waters which have become
its danger instead of its safety. A Norwegian steamer
came into Virginia Beach in the night, and by some mistake rammed its prow into the sand and was stranded
hard and fast. The experts, and all the "spurts," told
how to dislodge it from its grounded condition but the
mate knew that theirs were foolish counsels. He said,
"The breakers are not high, the sea is quiet; we will wait
and see what the tide will do." In thirty-six or forty-eight
hours a nine or ten foot tide silently, irresistibly flowed
in and lifted the big ship far above the sand; the engines
began to throb and the vessel gracefully sailed away
under its own power. All the tugs in Norfolk, Hampton
Roads, and Newport News could not have moved it an
inch. If churches and preachers would abandon them-

selves to the tides of grace, the incalculable powers of God's Holy Spirit, what wonders would be seen and felt in Zion!

The best news ever published is that men who do not deserve it may receive forgiveness as free as the water which they quaff from the meadow brook, or the air they breathe in mountain forests. A lost man said to me: "I am just not worthy to be saved." The answer given was: "Of course you are not worthy to be saved. You are only worthy and fit to be damned in an eternal Hell, because of your sin against a holy God, but the joy and the glory of it is that you do not have to be worthy, for He saves the unworthy and calls not the righteous (self-righteous) but sinners to repentance. Your sins will commend you to God's consideration if you will only repent and forsake them."

There is something in the Greek word for grace that fits nothing but the gospel of Christ. When John says: "The Word became flesh and dwelt among us full of grace and truth," he revealed a divine personality who emerged out of the unseen into the visible world. He told of one who consists of goodness, kindness, justice, and unselfish love. He is not one who merely bears an attribute of truth but one who *is* the truth; not one who can show love on occasion but one who is love in his very being and essence. When He took upon himself flesh and dwelt among us He was "the grace of God that bringeth salvation which hath appeared to all men"— (Titus 2:11).

One might say "the goodness of God that bringeth salvation," for surely God is at his best in seeking and saving that which was lost. We could say "the love of God which bringeth salvation," for it is the supremest demonstration of God's love; or "the mercy of God

which bringeth salvation," for salvation is the most
amazing exhibition of divine mercy. We could say "the
compassion of God," for He suffered for us in His death
on the cross. It is also the "righteousness of God which
bringeth salvation," for He "set forth Christ in His own
blood that He might Himself be just and the justifier of
him that believeth in Jesus." It is "the power of God
that bringeth salvation which hath appeared to all men,"
for the same power "which He wrought in Christ when
He raised Him from the dead and set Him at His own
right hand in the heavenly places" (Eph. 2) He exercises
when He calls a dead soul out of sin into life with Christ.

The grace of God, therefore, is the exercise and exhibition of all His holy attributes as these act in unity of
His divine person to effect the eternal salvation of His
people. Grace is God's dynamic love smiting sin, loving
the sinner, seeking reconciliation, cleansing man's conscience, nerving his arm in conflct, and sanctifying the
redeemed soul forever. Grace is cosmic in design, indi-
vidualistic in application, and perfect in its operation,
for it saves unto the uttermost all who come unto God
through Christ.

Grace is adequate to every condition. "My grace is
sufficient for thee, for my power is made perfect in
weakness." Note the singular, "sufficient for *thee*" (II
Cor. 12, 8, 9). In the last analysis everything must be
judged by its sufficiency. Dr. John S. Mackay said:
"There is no more ultimate criterion of truth than that
which satisfies one, but this something must continue to
satisfy in the most opposite circumstances of life. It
must satisfy when one's face is flushed with dawn and
when growing twilight casts its gloom over a furrowed
brow. It must satisfy when friends acclaim and when
friends forsake one. It must grow in intensity in the

measure in which it is shared with others. It must be an
element in the infinite satisfaction of God which holds
the universe together."

Grace was sufficient to tether and tame Paul when he
was riding in the madness of youth to persecute Christians
and hail both men and women to prison. Later he could
humbly confess: "By the grace of God I am what I am."
That divine power changed a raging persecutor into a
preacher of the Nazarene; made a sinner into a saint; an
opponent of Christ into His champion. It has done the
same for all who love the Lord. The supreme apolo-
getic of Christ is that He can take a bad man and make
a good man of him. Psychology cannot do this, neither
education, nor environment, nor modernistic theology.
There is no moral dynamic except that which emanates
from the cross that can accomplish such results. Grace
produces peace which passes all understanding; peace
which keeps the heart of believers until they shall see
Him face to face.

> "There is a fountain filled with blood
> Drawn from Immanuel's veins,
> And sinners plunged beneath that flood
> Lose all their guilty stains."

The conversion of Saul of Tarsus cannot be explained
apart from divine power that acted on him from without and changed him within. Opium smokers are not
cured by someone holding up before them an ethical
ideal. Inebriates are temporarily reformed by Keely
cures and Alcoholics Anonymous, but are cured only by
grace that works within and purifies the heart through
love. Incorrigible youth finds instruction in a house of
correction, but salvation comes in the house of the Lord.

"My grace is sufficient" is a promise for every day. The grind, the toil and moil, the dirt and difficulty of the common task are all included in this promise. The economic struggle is hard. The children's health and happiness must be guarded and provided for. Taxes must be paid and money for the winter's coal found. The battle is fierce but not futile. Grace is sufficient for all. Grace has a wonderful way of increasing income, suggesting helpful economies, multiplying thrift and energies, and firing hearts with indomitable and deathless courage which wrests victory from the jaws of defeat.

A fine looking, upstanding youngster had stolen money from a bank, been detected and convicted, and hurried away to prison. The pastor sat face to face with the bowed and broken hearted mother, who moaned: "Oh, if I could just take it all on myself and bear it for him and let him go free how glad I should be." What but grace can produce such sacrificial love, or offer comfort in such sorrow?

Grace can turn troubles into triumphs. How poor Paul would have been if God had answered his prayer directly by taking away his affliction without giving him superabundant grace to bear it. Is not all greatness achieved under handicaps? Spurgeon was hated and cartooned as few have been, and suffered agonies for years from gout. Robert Louis Stevenson was a lifelong invalid. Charles Lamb had the care of an epileptic sister as a precious life burden. In the kingdom of grace weakness means strength; dependence on God gives independence of men and circumstance. With grace the impossible becomes easy; faith is translated into fact; and to glory in one's infirmity is to have the power of Christ rest upon one, "overshadow" one like a tent as the Greek word signifies. The imagery in the apostle's mind must have been the Shekinah, the symbol of the glory of God that rested at times on the tabernacle.

And last, grace is sufficient for life's crises and life's translation when we meet the last enemy. "Precious in the sight of the Lord is the death of His saints." No life philosophy is worthy of respect that does not reckon with death. The aspiring soul of man looks beyond the grave and longs for some words of assurance. The soul is indomitable, persistent, sempiternal in its aspirations. It finds no satisfaction in an eternal negative. In the presence of death men are like children crying in the dark. They want to clasp a hand that is friendly and hear a voice which gives confidence. This is a universal feeling, and what is universal is true. This deepest heart-hunger cannot be laughed out of court by cynics or bowed out of the universe by agnostics. When a man of brilliant mind, mature culture, and world experience and observation through study and travel like Dr. E. M. Poteat is passing into the spirit land and says to those at his side: "Put this on my tomb: 'Forever with the Lord,'" only fools will scoff. Grace makes a sure footing for all its subjects who walk down the brink of the grave. "Since then the children are sharers in flesh and blood, he also himself in like manner partook of the same; that through death he might bring to naught him that had the power of death, that is the devil, and might deliver all them who through fear of death were all their lifetime subject to bondage." Grace enables men to go with death laughing because Christ hath abolished death and brought life and immortality to light through the gospel.

II

GRACE CHOOSES A PEOPLE

"Blessed be the God and Father of our Lord Jesus Christ, who blessed us with every spiritual blessing in the heavenly places in Christ, according as He chose us in Him before the founding of the world, that we should be holy and without blame before Him" (Eph. 1:1-4).

In November 1916 an enthusiastic crowd listened to the national election returns and shouted for joy or moaned their disappointment as the news was favorable or unfavorable to their presidential candidate. It was Wilson, Presbyterian elder, running for the second term, and Charles Evans Hughes, Baptist deacon, as the challenger. One doubts that two better and greater men ever asked the American people for their suffrage.

The Wilsonians made their campaign for their truly great man on the slogan: "He kept us out of war." The Hughes camp pleaded the outstanding legal ability, the fine record of a two-term Governor of New York, the distinguished record as Associate Justice of the United States Supreme Court, along with great learning and Christian character, as the worthy qualifications of their aspirant to the nation's highest office. The campaign was waged in a threatening war psychology that made people take sides. Neutrality was neither possible nor desirable, for great issues were involved. Intense rivalry produced a good deal of feeling, although both sides conceded the sterling qualities of the opposition candidate. To increase the excitement the two candidates were running neck and neck; therefore as many states were reporting late that night and the returns were shifting the advantage first to one side and then to the other it reminded one of a horse race where two great Man O'Wars were fighting to nose past that destiny string first. The country could not make a mistake by choosing either man, but strong party feeling wants "my man first of all."

Now the race is narrowed down to California, and that fluctuates back and forth to tantalize the excited crowd, but, presto, Hughes has taken a considerable lead that looks decisive, and he goes home and goes to bed, so happy that he could not sleep, one believes, in the thought that he was President of the greatest government God ever gave to men. At twelve o'clock that night the whole world thought Hughes was elected. The next morning the papers had got complete returns from California and announced that Wilson had shaved through with a small majority.

How disappointed Hughes must have been! How re-assured Wilson must have felt when the people, even though by small majority, had approved his policies. We all know how men will strive to be chosen to office and rejoice in victory. But these are withering laurel wreaths, on the heads of Marathon athletes, which fade and pass in the heat of a day. This is a crown which is dimmed with the using, but there is a diadem that grows brighter through all the increasing ages.

Paul tells in the great Scripture quoted above of a choice that reaches into the eternity back of us and into that which lengthens into the endless future. "According as He chose us in Him before the foundation of the world, that we should be holy and without blame before Him."

Note how the apostle leads up to this statement. "Blessed be the God and Father of our Lord Jesus Christ, who blessed us with every spiritual blessing in the heavenly places in Christ." "The God and Father of our Lord Jesus Christ" is an unusual expression. The active form of the Greek word for "blessed" here is used in the New Testament to apply only to God. It describes His intrinsic character, permanent and unchangeable. He is always blessed. There is a passive form of the same word which is applied to men to commend them for an act, or acts of well-doing. Hebrew students will recall *barak* which means "to bless" in the Old Testament, and is translated in the Septuagint by the Greek word used here.

God is ever and eternally blessed; and out of His blessed being He "blessed us with every spiritual blessing" *before* the doxology which is given to God. That runs true to form of all God's mercies. They antedate everything and everybody through His eternal purpose in Christ; and we are called upon to respond to His mercies with gratitude for His goodness. "Every spiritual blessing" comprehends the whole scheme and purpose of our complete salvation. The King James Version says: "With all spiritual blessing," which means much the same but the apostle makes it emphatic by saying "every spiritual blessing." The treasure house is full, and cannot be depleted by giving. The river of life never runs dry though all the myriads of men should come and drink. One eternal act of God's favoring mercy, indicated by Paul's Aorist tense, includes everything He has done for us and everything we shall ever need.

"In the heavenlies," Paul says, literally, without any word for "places." Therefore it could mean "the heavenly fellowship of the Christian life here," or all the blessings and heavenly experiences both here and hereafter. It comes to the latter anyway for "every spiritual blessing" means totality in the most absolute sense. Consequently everything that we experience in this life as Christians, and every ecstatic joy we shall experience through eternal fellowship with God and the saints in coming ages, is and shall be an integral part of the purchase Christ made for us in His redemptive sacrifice.

After this lofty doxology to the God and Father of our Lord Jesus Christ our author gives the cause, or the measure of all these blessings—the explication of them we might say, or of the purpose and activity of God which contains all these things. "According as He chose us in Him before the foundation of the world that we should be holy and without blemish before Him." The bigness of that purpose is bound to grow on you as you turn it over in mind.

His is a Deliberate Choice

There was no constraint on God but His benevolent nature. There was nothing in the subjects of the choice that made them desirable as they were, but only in what God could make of them was the reason for choosing them, and in the glory He could bring to Himself and to His Son.

It was an Individual, Personal Choice

It was not the selection of a nation or the dragooning of a multitude to some physical work or destiny. He did choose Israel to be a medium of revelation and instruction to other peoples, as well as a racial stock through whom the promised seed would come as the great Deliverer for Israel and the Gentile multitudes. But Paul is speaking here of God's eternal choice of His beloved family, made up of individuals, as our families are constituted of persons.

It was a Prescient Choice

Another very attractive feature of this choice is that it was prescient, intelligent, completely understood before hand. A choice which was made with a perfect knowledge of the individuals far in advance. Everything was known about the nature, genealogy, disposition, and environment. It is a very humbling thought to know that God knows all about us, but a very comforting experience to realize that knowing all about us He chose us nevertheless. We may have earthly friends who would turn away from us if they knew everything in our character and conduct but not so with God. If anything in the universe could arise to make Him cast us off He never would have chosen us. One does not know that a mother's love could stand such a test. One is thinking of a deacon in a Baptist church who became such a reprobate, so diabolic and infernal as a white slave trafficker, that when his dear old Christian mother was dying and they asked if she wanted them to wire Jim to come home she shook her head and said, "No." If she could have known all about him from the beginning she, no doubt, would have prayed God that she might never be the mother of such a son.

God's Purpose is All-inclusive

It carries responsibility as well as privilege. God permitted the United States to discover the atomic bomb. Moreover His purpose was good however much men may abuse rather than use it. Human ingenuity was active in the discovery and determinative so far as man was concerned but that was pursuant to, and dependent on, eternal purpose that runs through the universe. His purpose in material and spiritual matters is always benevolent and never malevolent. It was not accidental that this power came into hands of a Christian, peace-loving nation rather than a Godless and ruthless one.

The United States is now the financial, educational, medical, and mechanical center of the world. More than three-fourths of the world's automobiles pace American highways. There are more telephones in New York City than in France. We have come into this large place of power by the faith of our fathers and the purpose of God. What will this medical center of the world do to conquer disease and alleviate suffering? How will our gadgets be used for profitable living instead of enervating indulgence? Will our schools inculcate soundness of body, sanity of mind, and sincerity of soul and spirit, rather than the inflation of intellect, the enervation of the flesh, and the damnation of the soul? Will we discover God's power that is able to overcome and use the atomic bomb? Atomic energy is not the consummation of knowledge. Only tyros will write "*Ne plus ultra*" on the Hercules Pillars of exploration and think that all progress has been attained.

The Eternal Purpose Centers in Christ

Nothing is important apart from Him. Nothing can finally succeed which is opposed to him. Politics must be purified. The public press must be purged of its dominant world spirit. Society must be sobered and sanctified by the ethics of Jesus. Diplomats must cut out the "double tongue" meaning of that word and speak the truth. The home must be hallowed with a new sanctity of marriage and the responsibility of rearing children for God and not for greed. Churches must become

Christ-centered and not be controlled by social standards. Preachers must be slaves of Christ and not sycophants of money goons. One of the greatest perils to churches and preacher of this hour is quick, easy big money, the burden and tyranny of things, which is all contrary to the mind of Jesus. Money has a place in the work of the kingdom but God has never purposed to redeem the world by silver and gold and by the clever planning of men. "Not by might nor by power, but by my Spirit saith the Lord."

Nothing should operate out of harmony with Christ. Schools should teach because He is the source of all wisdom. Farms should grow corn because He is the bread of life. Bodies should be healed because He is the Great Physician. Nations should be friendly because He is the great Friend of all. All things should serve Him because He created them. They have their origin, their being and their destination in God. They are of Him, through Him, and unto Him. "Apart from Him, Christ, not even one thing came to pass that has come to pass," John asserts in the prologue of his Gospel.

Nothing exists that God did not know about in advance. Everything He created is good in essence and purpose. If God's plan could be seen in the large it would be a unifying power and the rallying point of all the nations. It would be recognized as constructive, not destructive, creative not consuming. Christ's intrinsic merit would dwarf and demonetize all other values. Souls would be more than salaries, character better than cash, manhood more than money.

Christ is the power that conserves and perpetuates the universe. Paul says in Colossians: "In Him all things consist," or hold together. He is likewise the moral and spiritual center of the universe. Nothing can be right which is contrary to Him, or permanent which rises up to oppose and defeat him. He is also the spiritual magnet that draws all spirits to Him.

A good story tells of a Christian man in an art gallery who came upon a great painting showing Christ on His cross. He looked and studied and meditated on the eternal significance of the deed the artist had portrayed. Then forgetful of where he was and of the presence of others in the museum he spoke out in ecstasy: "I love Him. I love Him." A man from another country who knew the language drew up and put his hand on the first man's shoulder and gazed at the picture and said, "I love Him, too." Then another and another came until a half dozen stood with their arms around one another, all saying in the common language of the Lord's Prayer: "*We* love Him." They had never met before but were a band of brothers because of the mystic tie in Christ that makes all believers one. He is the desire of all nations. To Him the land of Sinim stretches out her hands.

> "From Greenland's icy mountains
> To India's coral strands,
> Where Africa's sunny fountains
> Roll down her golden sands
> Salvation oh, salvation
> The joyful news proclaim
> Till earth's remotest nation
> Has learned Messiah's name."

In Christ national hatreds die and nations dwell in peace. At the cross the earth is level so that all can see and none can have the advantage. The manifold wisdom of God shall be made known, not only to men, but to powers and principalities in the heavenly places through the church. This is God's plan and purpose of the ages which cannot be defeated. Moreover He has already decreed it for "He put all things under His (Christ's) feet and gave Him (who is above all things) as head over all things to the church which is His body the fulness of the one who is filling all things in all" (Eph. 1:22, 23). The eternal purpose of God, then has been fixed from the ages, was promoted by the subjection of all things under the feet of our Lord and is being wrought out through the church, the body of Christ, at the present time and will continue to be effected through God's power by His body, until absolute perfection is realized by the fulness of all things in all the universe.

God's purpose centered in Christ who was a lamb slain before the foundation of the world. There is nothing inchoate, haphazard, fortuitous, uncertain about the purpose of God. There can be no misgiving, no defalcation, no miscarrying, no chance, no power of pomp, pride or circumstance that can defeat His eternal plan. If this be not true, the world is built on chance as uncertain as a throw of dice, and a man knows not whence he came, or whither he is going. Man is architect of his own fate only in the sense that he yields himself to this benevolent purpose or throws himself to the lions and ravening wolves for his own base destruction by refusing God's mercy. The inclination to choose the right is inspired and motivated by the loving divine purpose more than we poor sinners realize, for the preparation of the heart and the answer of the tongue are of the Lord.

> "I sought the Lord but afterwards I knew,
> He moved my soul to it who sought for me,
> It was not I that found, O Savior true,
> Nay, I was found by Thee."

All that God has done for us and all that He will do

for us here, all that He will do for us through increasing
ages in the heavenly places when He gives grace and
glory without measure, was included in His eternal purpose in Christ Jesus our suffering and risen Lord. Paul
puts the choice of God's people back in the eternities
by saying: "According as He chose us in Him before
the foundation of the world."

Paul used the word *"kosmos"* here, which refers
sometimes to the earth and sometimes to the whole created order, the universe. Since God is an eternal being how
could He act and choose His people except in eternity.
He chose them according to the counsel of His own will.
He wasn't conditioned, restrained, constrained, or limited
by anything or anybody outside of Himself. If He had
been He would not have been supreme; if He had been
limited man's salvation would have been at least and in
part of his own merit and power. Contemplating these
very things Paul exclaims: "O the depth of the riches
both of the wisdom and the knowledge of God! How
unsearchable are His judgments and His ways past tracing out! For who hath known the mind of the Lord?
Or who hath been His counsellor. For of Him, and
through Him, and unto Him are all things" (Rom. 11:
33-36).

Consummation of His Purpose

When all the work of Christ is finished the whole universe will be brought into subjection to God's will. Every stumbling stone shall be removed, every discord shall
be taken out of the music of the universe. But the ultimate purpose and maximum glory of God will be a completely redeemed and perfectly holy people. The supreme consummation of God's work as it pertains to
men is and shall be "that we should be holy and without

blame before Him." At best God's people here are far from holy. The work is only begun. The germ of the new and true life is in us but oh, how slowly it grows. What a handicap we have in the burden of a sinful body! How far we are from God's ideal! But the work will be finished. We shall be holy before Him. We shall be made fit to stand before Him so that He can find no vestige of sin, not a spot of impurity in us. This divine purpose can no more be defeated than can the tides be stayed, for it stands in the power of God and is wrought out through the Holy Spirit in the redeemed life of the believer.

Paul is talking about great things here. God's choice of His people. His eternal choice. His Christ-centered choice. His choice of them to the greatest destiny, that they should be holy before Him. They will be without blame. No slander can soil them. No lie the devil or their enemies may forge can touch them. No imperfection can be found in them in that day by the perfect eye of God Himself.

Are you not glad that He chose you knowing all about you? Doesn't your heart say: "Blessed be the God and Father of our Lord Jesus Christ, who according to His great mercy begat us again unto a living hope by the resurrection of Jesus Christ from the dead, unto an inheritance incorruptible, and undefiled and that fadeth not away, reserved in heaven for you who by the power of God are guarded through faith unto a salvation (which is) ready to be revealed in the last time"?

May "the God of our Lord Jesus Christ, the Father of glory give unto you the Spirit of wisdom and revelation in a full knowledge of Him; having the eyes of your heart enlightened, that ye may know what is the hope of His calling, what the riches of the glory of His inheritance in the saints, and what the exceeding greatness of His power to us -ward who believe according to that working of the strength of His might, which He wrought in Christ when He raised Him from the dead, and made Him to sit at His right hand in the heavenly places, far above all rule, and authority, and power and dominion, and every name that is named, not only in this world, but also in that which is to come, and He put all things in subjection under His feet, and gave Him to be head over all things to the church which is His body, the fulness of Him that filleth all in all."

III

GRACE REDEEMS THE CHOSEN PEOPLE

Ephesians 1:5-14

Solomon was a pretty gay "chap," a lover of pretty women and fine horses, in modern parlance. He is a hard nut to crack when you come to analyze his character. His cleverness is beyond doubt for he settled a quarrel between two women, a good one and a bad one. He evidently loved the garish and the gaudy both in society and in government. He burdened the people with high taxes to run his empire and left a son more unwise than himself in that regard, who said to his subjects: "My Father chastised you with whips but I will chastise you with scorpions" (I Ki. 12:14) and he kept his wicked promise which resulted in a division of his kingdom into Israel on the north and Judah on the south.

Solomon made a wise and humble request of the Lord when he became king—"Give thy servant therefore an understanding heart to judge thy people, that I may discern between good and evil; for who is able to judge this thy great people" (I Ki. 3:9). We are told (II Sam. 12:24) that God loved him when he was born. Later he was chosen to build the great temple that bore his name. God denied that privilege to David, who was a warrior and a man of blood.

Whatever you may think about Solomon and the wonderful part he played in the world's life you must concede that he was a big man of great ability and personality, who was wise and sagacious beyond comprehension, as well as weak and foolish, at times.

After uttering the prayer at the dedication of the temple, one of the greatest prayers in the Bible, Solomon plays the fool by giving his attention to many foreign women, who soon led him into the worship of their false gods. Because of this and of the unwise procedure of Rehoboam the kingdom was divided, although God permitted Solomon, for David's sake, to serve out his full reign.

But despite Solomon's mistakes he must have known how to repent and right himself, for Jesus refers to his splendor and magnificence and superior wisdom without any derogatory word. Son of Bathsheba, whom David took to wife after his act of adultery and murder, Solomon had rather a bad example from his Father.

Necessity of Repentance

Solomon is an impressive illustration of the fact that all men are dependent on the grace of God both for salvation of the soul and for the sanctification of the life. He did not make the grade so as to get into the honor roll of faith in Hebrews, along with many worthies, but he did find his way into the canon of Scripture with at least two books which have put all generations since his time in debt to him. After a long life through God's patience and merciful providence, he gave his final verdict and life philosophy—"This is the *end of the matter, all hath been heard: fear God and keep His commandments,* for this is the *whole duty of man.* For God will bring *every work into judgment* with every hidden thing whether it be good or bad" (Eccl. 12:13, 14).

His language echoes the memory of high living, flirting with women, and voluptuous indulgence which he knows to be displeasing to God. He knew that men have to be redeemed from their sins by the grace of God. He knew that God searches all hearts and will bring every dark deed and every sinful thought into judgment. "Be sure your sin will find you out" (Nun. 32:23) has not been blotted out of the Book. The searching eye of God is a fearful fact. Daniel Webster said that the most solemn thought that ever came into his mind was his responsibility to God.

Men are born in sin and must repent or die in their sins. They need redemption. The headlines of a daily paper prove that. The vocabulary of a dictionary with its vast majority of words of wicked, lustful, selfish, sinful connotations establishes man's depressed state, for out of the abundance of the heart the mouth speaketh. Every criminal court, every jail, chain gang, gallows, electric chair, is caused by sin. Wars, machine guns, booming cannon, bombing planes, atomic bombs, gas chambers, hand grenades; all the infernal death-dealing machines are the bitter fruit of sin from which men need redemption.

The voice of conscience which becomes alive at times with terrible might condemns the guilty. Shakespeare makes Richard the Third say:

"My conscience hath a thousand several tongues,
And every tongue brings in a several tale,
And every tale condemns me for a villain."

You might have thought that Herod would be deaf to every voice of conscience but when the works and fame of Jesus were resounding throughout Palestine guilty old Herod gasped with hot breath and pallid cheeks: "It is John whom I beheaded."

Years after graduation at college a woman returned her diploma to the President and wrote him that she did not deserve it, because she had cheated on an examination. A young preacher was conducting a meeting for me which was not succeeding as we felt that it should. One morning after a night of little sleep he said with suffering face and solemn voice: "This meeting is not going right and I am to blame for it. I cheated on that examination and then lied about it."

We cannot escape from life's memories. Conscience will be heard in the end; when it will burn like a scorpion with a thousand stings, and blister like a lash of cat-o-nine-tails. Pilate washed his hands and said: "I am innocent of the blood of this righteous man," (Matt. 27:24), but his sensible wife was troubled in a dream and sent to him the warning: "Have thou nothing to do with that just man for I have suffered many things this day in a dream because of him." Lady Macbeth looked at her bloody hand and raved: "Out, damned spot," but the stain remained and all the perfumes of Araby could not cleanse and sweeten her palm. Milton put into the mouth of Lucifer the words: "I myself am hell." The Scriptures, the dramatists, and the poets have all warned of the terrors of conscience. Even in hell there came to the rich man the bitter words: "Son, remember!"

There comes a time on the road to hell where the lights go out. It came to Judas when he received the sop and immediately went out; and John says, "And it was night." That is not chiefly an observation of the time of day, but a pronouncement of the doom of a soul. But whatever the guilt within, Christ can cleanse every stain and set the conscience free. A dear Christian woman told a minister that her mother always said that she had no unpleasant life memories. Would to God that the writer and the reader could say as much.

Paul says: "In whom we have redemption through his

blood the forgiveness of our trespasses according to the riches of his grace" (1:7). That is the only power in earth or in heaven that can forgive sin. The billions of dollars worth of gold buried in Knox County, Ky., cannot buy relief from pain, surcease from sorrow, or the salvation of a soul from death. There are atomic bombs enough at Oak Ridge, Tennessee, to blast and burn every chief city of any nation on earth, but they canot save one dying man or put out the flames of remorse or breach the gates of hell and set a damned spirit free. All the good deeds of every saint from righteous Abel to those of today cannot justify one soul before God. All the sacraments of man are nothing but filthy rags if presented to God for His perfect righteousness. But "Christ hath redeemed us from the curse of the law having become a curse for us, for it is written cursed is every one that hangeth on a tree."

Redemption has to do with a Person. Conning a creed and repeating a ritual have no power to save. There is no redemption apart from the Redeemer. The different noun and verb forms of this word occur about a hundred and twenty-five times in the Scripture. Where these words refer to salvation the action is ascribed to God, to Christ or to the Holy Spirit. It brings deep sorrow to look on multitudes who believe that good deeds, works of the law, or ordinances of the church can save them.

Men have so gloried in gadgets, worshipped scientific achievement and talked of the abundant (material) life, and fussed and fumed about security from want, and freedom from fear, that many believe that life consists of material abundance. It does not consist in things. "For what are men better than sheep or goats that nourish a blind life in the brain if knowing God they lift not hands in prayer both for themselves and those who call them friend"? "To do justly and love mercy and to walk humbly with thy God" is outmoded. Men do not need reformation but regeneration, not socialization but salvation, not a political ruler but a Redeemer. The slaughter of innocents, the traffic in woman's virtue, the ghastly murders of daily occurrence, the gangrenous corruption in national, state, and city government, which threaten the very existence of our republic, prove that redemption is our only hope. The scientists have frightened themselves with their engines of destruction and are now calling on the churches and preachers to save the country.

The newspapers call on the "parsons" to bolster the morale and the morals of the nation, then blast with lies and ridicule every minister who attacks their patron saint, the liquor business, which is the chief producer of crime. The only gospel for this day, and for everyday, is "Ye must be born again"—"Except ye repent ye shall all likewise perish"—"I am the way, the truth and the life; no man cometh unto the Father but by me."

Paul lived in a world as wicked as ours. Slavery, drunkenness, immorality, sodomy, exposure of infants, gladiatorial contests, brutal persecution of Christians, poverty and squalor, debasement of women to the lowest state of shame not only existed but were tolerated or promoted by organized society and government. But in daring and serene confidence the apostle announced a remedy for all the world's ills: "In whom we have redemption through his blood, the forgiveness of our trespasses, according to the riches of His grace."

Exposition of the Context

Note the marvelous way redemption is set forth in the context of verse 7. The origin of this plan of redemption goes back to eternity when He "chose us in Him before the foundation of the world." The words "in love" which the translation puts in verse four go better with the fifth verse. Putting these words in verse four makes "in love" refer to our love for God, a subjective idea, but this, one thinks, refers to God's love for us. We are not blameless before God because of our love for Him, but rather because of His love for us on account of which He gave His son to die for our sins; and we love God as a matter of gratitude because He first loved us. Our love to God is not the cause of our salvation, but a result of our saved relationship.

It makes no difference with the grammar whether you read "in love" with verse four or five, but theological reasons require that they go with verse five. Then we read: "In love having foreordained us unto the adoption of sons." Foreordination is the result of the benevolent purpose of God in choosing us unto eternal life in Christ; it is the enabling act, so to speak, to put His purpose and choice into effect. It is not something mechanical and cold as ice to freeze human affection; but something warm as the heart blood of divine love which is exerted in our eternal favor; an essential part of his loving eternal decrees which provide for our sonship and guarantee certain, unchangeable, eternal salvation of all believers in Christ. Foreordination has a distinct purpose and objective. He foreordained us unto adoption of sons, and the sonship comes about through Jesus Christ, and it is unto God. He eternally chose us, and foreordained us to sonship through Christ unto Himself, for Himself. We are His own, the people of His hand and the sheep of His pasture. This all was according to the good pleasure of His will. He was under no constraint but the forwardness of His eternal benevolence. There was no merit or reason on our part for His doing it. Moreover, it was unto the praise of the glory of His grace where-with He "graced" (Paul uses grace as a verb) us in the Beloved. Then the author, with a present tense, states the great matter: "In whom we have the redemption through His blood the forgiveness of sins according to the riches of His grace."

He says: "*The* redemption"; the redemption that had been promised through the Messiah; the redemption which had been hoped for and expected through all the centuries of prophetic Scriptures; *the* redemption that marks it out as true and faithful from all other schemes and theories of redemption which are deceiving and deadly; *the redemption* by way of pre-eminence which sets it forth as the only one and excludes all others from consideration.

The Meaning of Redemption

The Greek word for redemption is a compound made up of a word which means the price paid for a slave, and a preposition which means "from", "away from". It is the Ablative idea of separation, or "removal away from." In the natural state men are servants, slaves of sin. In another place (Rom. 6:17, 18) the apostle says: "But thanks be to God, that whereas ye were servants of sin, ye became obedient from the heart to that form of teach-ing whereunto ye were delivered; and being made free from sin, ye became servants of righteousness." Also in Galatians three thirteen, it is said: "Christ redeemed us from the curse of the law, having become a curse for us; for it is written, cursed is everyone that hangeth on a tree." In the phrase "A curse for us" Paul uses a preposi-tion which means "in our behalf, in our place"—plainly the teaching of substitution, or vicarious atonement. Christ's death was not merely an exhibition of God's love, although it is the greatest proof of His love. There was a necessity for His death. "Thus it is written that the Christ should suffer and rise again from the dead the third day" (Luke 24:46). The death of Christ was a full and just equivalent of all the outraged law of God required of the sinner. He did really take the sinner's place, bearing his guilt and dying in his stead.

As indicated above, the word "redemption" carries the idea of setting a slave free from his bondage. The word for redemption here, and commonly in the New Testament, is *apolutrosis*. The Lexicon defines the verb, from which this noun is derived, "To release on payment of ransom; to redeem for money." Thayer defines the noun: "A releasing effected; redemption; deliverance, liberation procured by payment of a ransom."

Redemption does not mean that God is like a silly father who puts his hand in the fire just to show that he loves his child. Christ did not hurl himself to death in the flood in order to make known His love to a man who was watching in perfect safety from the shore. Man was drowning in sin and Christ risked and sacrificed His life to rescue him. The moral balance had been destroyed by sin and had to be restored by someone suffering the penalty of transgression.

In Mississippi a house was burning and nearly ready to fall in, when the father of the family rushed up and started to enter the building. Friends laid hold on him to restrain him from what seemed sudden death. He freed himself like a giant and darting into the flaming structure, felt and fumbled his way through the choking smoke to his bedroom and dropped his little child out of a low first story window, where friends outside could reach and remove it from danger. Then he jumped out himself. Then a shout of acclaim arose for a deed of heroism, which had seemed to the crowd an act of supreme folly. When the moral purpose was revealed the act was the most natural thing; yea, inevitable because necessary to satisfy a universal moral law. So God was acting in perfect consonance with the moral and spiritual character of the universe when He sent Christ to be a propitiation for our sin. There was moral necessity for the atonement growing out of the benevolent character of God. Either the whole race must die under the broken law, or God must save them by declining to punish sin, and thereby become immoral, or He must save them by putting their sins on the "Lamb of God that taketh away the sin of the world." God chose the last.

In the Hebrew Scriptures the redeemer was called the "Goel", the nearest of kin. The nearest of kin would rise up to avenge one's wrongs, or to buy and win back an estate that had been alienated from an orphan child or lost by the rightful owner. Redemption is an actual, *"bona fide"* transaction of setting the sinner free from his bondage. In 1944 during the second World War the Germans had taken as prisoners several hundred English sailors and had them deep in the hold of a ship in Norway. One night an English ship slipped into the fjord, overpowered the guards and lifting one of the hatches shouted: "Are there any Englishmen down there," and the Tommies rolled out by the hundreds to join their buddies, their redeemers, on deck.

A Scriptural example is Lot, who had been captured by the kings confederate with Chedorlaomer. He was in slavery. His life was in danger. Abraham, his uncle and good friend, who had not been turned away from Lot by Lot's greedy choice and bad conduct, marshalled his military men, and by an onslaught as impetuous as that of Cromwell and his Ironsides, wrested Lot from their control and brought him back to freedom. He thereby became Lot's "Goel", or Redeemer (physical of course). That was man's condition. He was sold under sin, and Christ sets him free through His sacrifice.

A Present Redemption

With a present tense of his verb Paul says: In whom we "have redemption"; we have it now and go on having it. He says that we have it in Christ. He says that we have it through Christ's blood. He says that redemption is the forgiveness of sins. He says that the measure of this redemptive forgiveness of sins is according to the riches of God's grace. He says that with this amazing grace He abounded unto us in all wisdom and prudence, or judgment, when He made known to us the mystery of His will according to His good pleasure. He says that this was all purposed in Christ unto a dispensation of the fullness of the times or seasons. He assures us that it was all done for the purpose of summing up in one headship all things both in heaven and on the earth in Christ. How wonderful to have this redemption now. Unlike fire insurance it is active now so that you need not to be burned out to receive benefit. Different from life insurance it brings blessing in life and death and goes not to another. It is a present possession. Its merit is the inestimable merit of Christ's death. It stands in the power and decree of God and not in human weakness. It was accomplished once for everyone who believes on Jesus and is never repeated—doesn't need to be.

We were slaves but now are free in Christ. We were children of wrath and He made us children of God. We were in a prison house dark as a dungeon and He brought us out and set us on a hill of light and glory.

Sin is slavery, hence Paul uses the word for the price

of liberation of a slave. There is great degradation in slavery. It signifies arrogant lords, grinding servitude, debased ideals, galling chains, and foul and fetid prisons. It means lost liberties, libidinous habits, and a sinful state from which men cannot even desire freedom without outside aid to quicken and qualify them for a nobler existence. How marvelous it is to be now delivered from all this only the redeemed can know. If there is nothing for men to be delivered from the death of Christ was an impertinence, a work of supererogation. The big question with men, and seemingly with God, has ever been how can God be just and the justifier of sinners? The solution of this question is that God set forth Christ in His blood that He might be just and the justifier of them that believe in Jesus (Rom. 3:25, 26).

Men have made a sorry spectacle of themselves in their rebellion against God. In willfully asserting their independence of God they have publicized their allegiance to the devil. In their boasted independence they have exchanged the light of revelation for the darkening counsels of human reason. They are plagued with leopard's spots of which they are unconscious.

Sin is a disease which medication cannot cure, a dye which Fuller's soap cannot wash out. "For though thou wash thee with lye and take thee much soap yet is thine iniquity marked before me saith the Lord Jehovah" (Jeremiah 2:2). To be freed from such a state and made forever immune from its dominion is redemption. God has set Himself the task of taking a race of slaves and liberating them, washing them through regeneration and sanctification of the Spirit, adopting them as His children and making them a righteous, victorious army marching under His banner of peace and love, fighting the good fight of faith. This deliverance was accomplished potentially and fully by Christ on the cross; and it becomes available to all those who repent and trust the Saviour.

The Price of Redemption

Speaking of his Roman citizenship the chief Captain in Jerusalem said to Paul: "With a great price obtained I this freedom," and the apostle proudly replied: "But I am a Roman born." There is a citizenship that money cannot buy. It comes only by a birth of the Spirit. Redemption was wrought not by silver and gold but by the precious blood of Christ. It was set forth in type by Abraham's offering of Isaac. The passover lamb in Egypt illustrates the deliverance and safety we have in Christ. The daily sacrifice in the temple spoke of the One who would offer Himself and then enter into the most holy place and obtain eternal redemption for us. Baptism heralds His death for our sins and His resurrection for our justification. The Lord's supper presents His broken body, which is both the source of our life and the daily food for our souls.

We exult in the freedom of redemption. We invite men to come and buy wine and milk without money and without price, and joyfully they may all do so. Ah, but that does not mean that redemption cost no one anything. It must have been a lonely day in heaven when Christ left on His earthly mission. God hid His face in darkness when the Savior died on the cross. The Lord went through unutterable agony when He said: "My soul is exceeding sorrowful even unto death"—"Father, if it be possible let this cup pass." The Scripture never promises salvation through the life of Christ, perfect and adorable as He was. Once it is said: "We are saved by His life," but the context shows that it was His resurrection life. He had gone through the experience of the cross. Salva-

tion is attributed to the suffering of the Lord. "When I
see the blood I will pass over you," was the promise of
safety from the destroying death angel in Egypt. It is
the same hope for our salvation for He is our passover
according to Paul. Christ has "made peace by the blood
of His cross." While a schoolboy, one read some Greek
author, who told the story of two armies who fought and
then made a peace treaty. When the compact was written and accepted by both sides, their leaders opened their
veins and let blood into a basin; then dipped their swords
in the blood and signed the document pledging their
lives sacredly to keep the treaty.

So Christ has made peace by the blood of His cross;
and we are saved through His death, and sanctified by
the word of "Christ Jesus who was made unto us wisdom
from God, and righteousness and sanctification and redemption." Dr. Berry and Dr. J. H. Jowett rode together on the train in England one day and Dr. Berry
told Dr. Jowett this story. He said: "When I was a
young preacher I did not believe that we are saved
through the blood or by the death of Christ. I thought
that we are saved by moral ideals and good works. There
came to my house one night a poor girl who said 'Are
you Doctor Berry?' Being told that I was, she said: 'My
mother is out and we want you to come and get her in.'
'Why don't you ask the police, they will help you,' I
responded. 'Oh, it is not that!' the poor thing said. 'She
is not drunk as you suppose, but she is dying, and she is
out of heaven and we want you to come and get her in.'
'Aren't there ministers nearer to you?' I rejoined. Then
she said: 'Yes Sir, there are, but we wanted you if you
would come.' 'All right,' I assented, 'I will go with you.'"
He followed the child to a pub where downstairs there
was drunkenness, revelry, and hideous sin; while upstairs
in a bare room on a bed of straw was a sinful, scarlet,

dying woman. He sat down by her and told her of the beautiful life of Jesus, and read to her from the Sermon on the Mount and said: "Now you obey the wonderful moral teaching of Jesus and imitate His spotless life and God will save you." The woman stared at him from her dying eyes and said: "Preacher, that may be all right for some, but it is no good for the like of me, for I am a *sinful* woman and I am dying, preacher." Berry said that it flashed on him that he had no message for the sinful, dying woman. He said: "I went back to the days of my childhood and remembered how my mother taught me about God's Son who came to earth and lived a sinless life, and died on the cross for our sins, and beginning there I preached to the dying woman, Jesus, God's Son, who died on the cross for her." Then he slapped Jowett on the shoulder and said: "Jowett, I got her in; and that is not all, Jowett, I got myself in, for I had never before known the sweetness and power of salvation until I preached unto the woman, Jesus Christ, God's sacrifice for sin."

That is the only way you can "get them in." From country communities, cotton mill chapels, mission stations, rescue centers, city churches, university centers, one has for more than fifty years seen them come in through the blood, and go forth to live and love, and sing and serve in the name of the Lord.

"I saw the cross of Jesus when burdened with my sin,
I sought the cross of Jesus to give me peace within;
I brought my soul to Jesus; He cleansed it in His blood;
And in the cross of Jesus I found my peace with God."

The Results of Redemption

The results of this redemption are manifold and mighty. One result is that all sins are forgiven—yes, *all* sins of condemnation are forever removed from the believer. Redemption *is* the forgiveness of sins as Paul says. The sinner's sins are unto condemnation. The believer's sins after he is saved are not unto condemnation, but he will be chastised for his disobedience; and the rod may fall heavily upon him but it will be unto correction and not unto destruction.

Believers' sins are removed from them as far as the east is from the west. They are "blotted out as a thick cloud." They are cast into the depths of the sea. They are remembered no more forever. You stand by the rail of a ship and drop a nickel into the sea. It goes down and down, three miles, ten miles, twenty miles and on so deep that sounding lines break or are not long enough to sound the immeasurable depth of the ocean. That nickel has disappeared forever, never to be seen again by mortal eyes—unless a mighty earthquake should upheave the whole ocean and change the bottom of the sea to exposed land. That is what has become of the Christian's sins. They are remembered no more forever by God Himself.

The measure of redemption is according to the immeasurable riches of God's grace. This grace He caused to abound unto us in every wisdom and prudence; and made known the mystery of His will according to His good pleasure. This was purposed in Christ. It was unto a dispensation, or plan, of the fullness of the times. It was at the right time in the confluent streams of divine purpose and love, conjoining with the stream of history. The design of it was to sum up all things in Christ that He might be the head and have universal dominion unto the glory of God the Father. In Christ God made us His heritage, or property. Moreover He made it certain for He predestinated us according to the purpose of Him who is working all things after the counsel of His will.

Paul did not say "In whom we have obtained an inheritance." That is a great idea which the King James version expresses, but is not what the apostle is talking about here. He said: "In whom we were made a heritage"— we know that is what he said for he put his verb in the passive voice. It is impossible to translate his word which is in the passive voice, "We have obtained." This relation to God is unto the end that we should be unto the praise of His glory.

The crowning result of redemption which Paul presents is the sealing of all believers by the Holy Spirit, and the word for "Holy" carries strong emphasis. He is God's Spirit; and He is glorious, and awful in holiness. God eternally purposed our salvation, eternally chose us in Christ Jesus, called us with effectual calling, redeemed us with the precious blood of the Lamb slain from the foundation of the world; and sealed us with the Holy Spirit of promise. The Holy Spirit sealed and approved our salvation. This is an earnest and a pledge of complete and eternal redemption of body and soul and spirit— all that Christ bought in His agonies of body and soul on the cross. An earnest is an advance payment which guarantees all the rest shall be forthcoming. It is a pledge that the contract price will all be paid. Sealing is an attestation of ownership, the writing of the owner's name on the property. It is a guarantee and declaration against the property's ever going into alien hands. It is an ineffaceable mark by which the property can be identified. The winnowing angels will seal the servants of God on their foreheads when the Lord comes in His glory.

If you should doubt the reality of your redemption remember that it was wrought out in the bodily and spiritual travail of Christ on His cross. If uncertain about its value remember that it is priced by the riches of His grace. If you fear that it may not last remember that it was purposed and planned from eternity and projected on the merit of Christ into eternity. If you feel that your sins are too great to be forgiven then remember that where sin abounded grace did much more abound. If sin came in like a flood, grace came in like a tidal wave to sweep it all away. If you think that you are not worthy to be saved, you are entirely correct, for you are worthy only to be condemned and banished from God, but know that He came not to call the righteous but sinners to repentance. If you tremble lest He cast you off then know that you are a child and that a son abideth in the Father's house forever.

"We often speak of Jesus as Redeemer for His work was redemption work, concerned with redeeming men for the society of their fellows. He put His healing hand on the source of their loneliness and restored them to community. But this was not His chief concern. His chief concern was restoring them to fellowship with God. Men are made for community, but men are made for God. It is a burden to lose the fellowship of men, but it is hell to lose the fellowship of God" (Wm. C. Hart in *Pulpit Digest*).

IV

THE SPIRIT OF GRACE ENABLES US TO KNOW

Ephesians 1:15-23

A mob dragged a man out of the temple in Jerusalem one day and stoned him to death. They had heard him speak in the council; and fastening their eyes on him they saw his face as it had been the face of an angel. His speech was irresistible. The hearers had to accept it or kill the man who made it. They chose the latter. They gnashed their teeth, stopped their ears against Stephen's rebuke of their sins, screamed like madmen, rushed upon him with the fury of demons and cast him out of the city and stoned him as he was asking the Lord not to lay their sin to their charge.

Stephen's vision of heaven and of Jesus standing on the right hand of God, his shining face, his faith and fortitude, and prayer for his enemies during his martyrdom were miracles of the Holy Spirit. In his life he spoke with a Spirit they could not resist and in his death he had the presence and the power of that Spirit which their hate could not destroy. All believers have the same Spirit who gave Stephen victory in life and in death.

Paul prays: "That the God of our Lord Jesus Christ, the Father of glory may give unto you the Spirit of wisdom and revelation in a correct knowledge of Him." The Holy Spirit makes the Christian calling a reality in Christian experience; enables the believer to know the riches of the glory of God's inheritance in the saints;

and the exceeding greatness of His power toward us who believe.

The great things in this prayer are so compact and comprehensive that we must look at them carefully through exposition of the context before we dwell on the three things that Paul says he wants us to know.

When Paul says: "For this cause I too" he could refer to verse three and mean that he was thinking of the whole counsel and eternal choice of God which he first mentioned. More likely he is thinking of "ye also," verse thirteen, and of the sealing of the Holy Spirit. That makes a good balance between "ye also" and "I too on my side."

Good news had come to the faithful missionary about the Christians in the region of Ephesus. Their faith in the Lord Jesus and their attendant love toward all the saints opened his mouth in unceasing thanksgiving in their behalf. How we all felt the same way about Dr. Wallace in China, who was seized by the Communists and done to death in the most brutal manner. Before we knew of his tragic end his faith and love of the brotherhood were recounted in every conversation about him. When he was gone these virtues remained the imperishable memorial of a life that can never die.

Paul adds: "making mention in my prayers," thinking, perhaps, of the faith and love toward all the saints so manifest in the brotherhood of the Ephesian area. It is hopeless and abominable egotism to inform the Lord about our own good qualities; but we are on safe Biblical and apostolic ground when we mention, even in our prayers, the faith, and love, and sufferings of our Christian compatriots who counted not their lives dear unto themselves; and suffered all and gave all to Him who became obedient even unto death on a cross.

Again the three names of Jesus, that Paul loves to repeat, are given—"our Lord Jesus Christ." He is Lord supreme in power and authority over all flesh and all creation. He is Jesus, bone of our bone and flesh of our flesh. He is the Christ, the Messiah, the Anointed One, foretold by the law and the psalms and the prophets of old. In repeating these three names the author may have in the background of his thought the dangerous heresy known as Gnosticism. This was a syncretism, or rather hodgepodge, of oriental mysticism, dualism, heathen cults, with a mixture of Plato's philosophy more or less perverted, and some of the teaching now propagated by "Christian Science," with some gloss of Christian teaching included. This mixture, mainly of heathen origin, was offered as a substitute for the Christian gospel; and was proclaimed and propagated by some of the most astute and intellectual men of the early centuries. Its advocates thought their philosophical speculations would dilute Christianity and make it pleasing to the intellectuals of that day. This was the first giant heresy that threatened the very existence of Christ's church, and Paul met it head on, and by his teaching and writings broke its power; although the reptile wriggled through several centuries before its demise. Even yet, as instanced by "Christian Science," promoters of fantastic heresies go back to the Gnostics and exhume some of their bones, on which those who are wise above what is written may gnaw.

Space will not permit extended discussion of Gnosticism, one of the most complex, confused, and satanic schemes ever devised against the church, but roughly classified its devotees consisted of two main divisions. They were the Docetic Gnostics, and the Cerinthian Gnostics. The Greek word "docetic" means "to *seem*

to be, not real." The Docetics taught, therefore, that
the body of Jesus was not real, but only a phantom. The
Cerinthians, followers of Cerinthus, on the other hand,
said that the body of Jesus was real, but that He was not
divine. They claimed that the Christ spirit came on Him
at His baptism and deserted Him at the cross. They all
thought that knowledge was sufficient in religion, without revelation, hence they harped constantly on "gnosis," (Greek word for knowledge) and claimed to have
superior, and esoteric knowledge, and that they, therefore, were the only true interpreters of Christianity. Together the two branches of Gnosticism denied everything that is fundamental about the Lord. You can see
the point in Paul's giving him the three titles. He is
Lord, the Supreme One, Jesus the Man of Flesh, and
Christ, the Anointed One, the Messiah who was to come.

The liberals of today who deny the Virgin Birth of
the Lord follow the Cerinthian Gnostics and teach that
Jesus was only a man, but that he was given some special
endowment which made him "unique" (they love that
word) and qualified him to be a supreme example for
us to follow. They do not believe that Christ suffered
to put away sin; in fact, that was unnecessary because
there is nothing in the nature of sin and in man's guilt
that God cannot pass over without exacting a penalty.
Therefore the death of Christ came about from circumstances which He could not control; His death was that
of a martyr to truth, like unto that of Socrates. It was
an exhibition of God's love, without any matter of
justice involved. However, anybody may evaluate this
heresy in its ancient or modern manifestation let it be
understood in all candor and truth that such teaching
finds no basis whatever in the New Testament.

Paul probably makes further reference to this heretical

system when he prays that God may "give unto you the Spirit of wisdom and revelation in an accurate (or full) knowledge of Him." He is saying to the worldly wise ones that human knowledge is not enough, that men cannot find out God by ratiocination. The world by wisdom knew not God. Men must have the clear light of revelation which comes from the Spirit of God and through the Spirit-inspired word of God.

The Greek word for "accurate, (or full) knowledge" is instructive. The heretics majored on "gnosis," knowledge, but Paul puts a preposition to the word and makes it "epignosis," which means additional, more, accurate, full knowledge. He is saying to them, "You talk much about knowledge but your supreme need is more knowledge, or correct knowledge about God to correct your partial and partisan knowledge." Of course, that is not said alone to those schismatics. It is essential for all who would come to God and understand the nature and grace of God to have correct knowledge.

"The Spirit of wisdom and revelation" has been much discussed. Because the word for spirit does not have the definite article some have said the clause should be rendered "a spirit of wisdom and revelation"; that Paul was praying that they might have a spirit that would make them wise to understand revelation. But spirit had come to be a proper name for the Holy Spirit and names may be used without the article unless the context should require it. Moreover "spirit" here is followed by a Genitive case, and Greek students know that that may make a noun definite. But a more important reason than these matters of grammar is that there does not seem to be any example in the New Testament where the power of making revelation was given to men. That is a function that belongs only to God through His Spirit. Paul says in another place: "All Scripture is God-breathed," and he used the word "theopneustos," which consists of the word for "God," and a form from the same root as "spirit"—which in classic Greek means "air, wind," or "breath," as well as the life principle in man. These reasons and the context of the word here all add up to practical certainty that we should read the clause "the Spirit of wisdom and revelation." Only the Holy Spirit can impart to them and to us a true and accurate knowledge of God, so that we can know "what is the hope of His calling; what is the riches of His glory in His inheritance in the saints; what is the exceeding greatness of His power toward us who believe."

Another marvelous mercy here which is a revelation that becomes a reality in Christian experience is "the eyes of your heart being enlightened," (or illuminated). There can be no reasonable doubt that the King James Version is wrong in reading "the eyes of your understanding." Paul, according to preponderating authorities, used the Greek word for heart, which we meet with in "cardiac," "pericardium," and "carditis." "The eyes of the heart" means much more than "the eyes of the understanding." "The eyes of the heart" includes the whole mental, moral and spiritual man—not just the understanding. Why does a tired mother sleep through a raging storm that bowls over trees and makes the house tremble, and dashes sheets of rain against the wall, but wakes instantly when the baby fetches a dangerous cough as if pneumonia was coming? It is because she listens with the heart while she sleeps. After the busiest day in the life of Jesus, according to the details in the record, He lay down on the "cushion" in the rear of the little ship and went to sleep. A violent storm which frightened the sea-faring disciples never wakened the Master. But their cry of distress brought Him instantly to the deck with His lordly command to the waters: "Be muzzled," and they became as docile as a muzzled mastiff led by the strong hand of its owner. Jesus heard with His heart. No human cry ever escapes Him because His heart is so concerned for us. The "heart" includes the mental, moral, and volitional makeup of the human personality.

That is exactly the work of the Holy Spirit, to give full knowledge to believers, and to do this He enlightens the eyes of the heart. The all-wise and blessed Holy Spirit is the only one who can light the candle of knowledge and kindle the flame of affection in redeemed persons, and enable them to understand, and cause them to give deepest devotion to the redemptive purpose and soul-subduing love of our Father God in Christ Jesus our Lord.

The Hope of His Calling

What is the end or purpose of this illumination which the Holy Spirit will send into our heart? It is "That you may know," with that "accurate" knowledge of God, "what is the hope of His calling, and what is the riches of the glory of His inheritance in the saints, and what is the exceeding greatness of His power toward us who believe."

Anyone who reads Greek cannot miss the force and purpose of Paul's construction of this great sentence. In all three members of the sentence he uses "what is." "What is the hope"; "what is the riches of the glory"; "what is the exceeding greatness." Moreover in all three members of the sentence he uses "His." "The hope of His calling. The riches of the glory of His inheritance.

The exceeding greatness of His power." He must have meant the sentence as a unity with all three parts of it referring to God's activity in "calling," saving and sanctifying and glorifying His people for His eternal praise.

"The hope of His calling." Here we must remember that Paul's use of "calling" means electing, or choosing. With him "the called" are "the elect." His calling embodies and inspires the marvelous and blessed Christian hope. But that is not so much what Paul is after here. He is talking about the eternal purpose of God's electing His people to eternal life through Christ Jesus and is praying that the Holy Spirit may give them an understanding, full knowledge, of God's purpose in their calling, and of the riches of the glory of His inheritance in them. This is made as plain as a sign post in the eleventh verse of this first chapter where the apostle says: "In Him, in whom we *were made* a heritage having been predestined according to the purpose of the one who is now working all things according to the counsel of His will." We are not in doubt here. Paul put his verb in the passive voice. We were not acting but being acted upon by His will. Of course all Christian and heavenly inheritance comes through Christ but that is not what he is saying here. He is saying that we are God's heritage, God's property, God's wealth. "The Lord's portion is His people"—a familiar idea in the Old Testament. And that does not apply just to the Jews. All God's people are His heritage.

This Scripture is not talking so much of what we have in Christ or in God, but what God has in His people. It is very humbling and should put lips in the dust to say it, but God thinks He has a very great and rich inheritance in His redeemed people. God is greatly pleased with our obedience, and our service which He can empower and cause to enhance His glory, but we are much more to Him than all we do or can do. A father's son is much more precious to him than all the son has or all the son's labors.

We are bound to think that beloved Paul was not thinking so much of the Christian's calling and hope and what he is going to get out of it, as he was dwelling on God's calling according to the election of His grace; and how it would eternally enhance and glorify God's inheritance in the people of His love. The greatest thing in Christian life is not what we can do for God, proper and valuable as that is, but what we will let God do for us in forming the image of Christ in us. His greatest hope and pleasure is that we shall be conformed to the image of His Son. That is the hope of His calling, not our calling, which this inspired man wants us to have a full knowledge of, an accurate knowledge which the Holy Spirit alone can give us and will give us if we open our hearts to His illuminating wisdom.

By "calling" here Paul means God's election. Colossians 3:5; 1 Tim. 6:12; Rom. 1, 6, 7 seem to carry this meaning, and Romans 8:28-30 is unmistakable in this respect. "And we *Know* that to them that love God all things work (are working, present tense) together for good even to them that are called according to His purpose." But Paul uses the article and says "to them that are *the* called according to His purpose." He proceeds: "For whom He foreknew, also (He) foreordained to be conformed to the image of His Son that He might be the first born (from the dead) among many brethren. And whom He foreordained these also He called; and whom He called these He also justified; and whom He justified these also He glorified." In every main verb in the sentence (Vs 29, 30) Paul used a timeless aorist tense showing what God did in eternity. "These also He glorified," the last clause in the sentence, which could not possibly have come to pass already in God's people, conditions and rules the whole sentence. The sentence tells the story of God's eternal purpose and decree concerning His people and establishes the fact that to Paul the "called" are the eternally "elect"; that to "know" accurately the hope of His calling is to know the significance and purpose and outcome of God's choosing His people. There is cosmic significance in God's choosing a people to bear His name, to be conformed to the image of His blessed Son, to live as God's children and representatives before a sinful world, and to be glorified finally with Christ, and be associated with Him in the judgment of those who counted His blood of the covenant an unholy thing.

That eternal calling and God's perfecting it in His people will affect the whole universe; and every created being, men, angels, and demons—even inanimate nature itself—will feel the impact of it for glory or despair. The whole creation groans and travails in pain together waiting for the adoption, that is the redemption of the body. The hope of His calling is to change that and every other sorrow and limitation and bring to God eternal glory for a planned and perfected redemption of His people, and for the restoration of justice and holiness throughout the universe that has been blighted with blasphemy and soiled by sin.

To Know the Hope of His Calling

Now what is it that Paul wants us to know, that God wants us to know? What Paul prayed is what God desires for our lives. The first thing he wants us to know is the hope of His Calling. It need not be stated that the apostle is writing to Christians. He is addressing those who have already been effectually called by the Spirit. His regular use of "called" means the elect, as observed above. This is one of the most profound and spiritual prayers ever offered in behalf of believers. The humble spirit of wisdom which the Holy Spirit alone can give is requisite to understanding the hope of His Calling. Even a scientist of cocky spirit is a monstrosity. Unprejudiced, passionate attitude toward the truth is a condition of all learning. The gates of knowledge open softly to the touch of rosy fingers of unselfish love. Even Christians need to have their eyes opened by the light of the Spirit. If we of the Lord's house cannot learn the difference between thought and things, between men and money, between souls and sales, between spirituality and spiritualism, between revivals and rantings, between religion and rubrics, between prayers and paternosters, then how can the untutored masses ever sense the eternal values of the human spirit? We have almost forgotten that spiritual things must be spiritually discerned—or Spirit-imparted.

How little we know about what it means to be a Christian! We grope in the twilight, we stumble and feel our way, we see men as trees walking, we limp and loiter instead of running as the hind. We are toddling children and doddering grand-daddies rather than robust athletes and brave soldiers marching to conquest.

Ask the run-o-mine Christian the meaning of his faith and you will see his blank stare and hear his inane reply. Nothing definite, clearcut and purposeful comes from his lips. The apostle wants us to know the high hope that beats in the heart of conquerors. In another place he sets forth one objective of his calling when he said: "That I may lay hold on that for which I was laid hold on by Christ Jesus." Is not the supreme privilege and duty of the Christian calling to be, and to apprehend and achieve the same things in our life that Christ purposed in choosing us for himself? What did God have in mind in His Calling? Was it not that He was pleased to show mercy on the lowly and unworthy? Did He not mean to demonstrate his power to take sinners and make saints; to overthrow the plans of evil and turn them into a means of blessing? Did He not purpose to make righteousness, peace and brotherhood dominant in the universe instead of sin, hate, discord, and war?

What is the hope of His Calling? There is something here so colossal that we cannot measure it, so high we cannot scale it, so valuable we cannot price it, so expansive we cannot explore it, so beautiful we cannot describe it. We are finite struggling to comprehend the infinite.

To understand the Calling we must know more of Him who called us. To that end the apostle prayed that He would grant unto us the Spirit of wisdom and revelation in a correct knowledge of Him. Only the Spirit can give that correct or full knowledge of God. The bigness and the beauty, the mercy and the might, the justice and the goodness, the concern and the compassion, the righteousness and the reign, the paternity and the patience, the solicitude and the plenitude, the love and the long-suffering of our God are so amazing and so divine that they are past comprehension unless and until the Spirit of revelation makes them real to our hearts.

One would appeal to the reader's experience. Have you ever known the reality and immediate presence of

God except when the Spirit taught you? Have you had a revelation of your sin—yes, since you have been a Christian—so pungent and powerful that you felt that you should die if your depravity was further revealed to your conscience? Then have you been conscious of the all-inclusive, overwhelming, forgiving love of God that swept away all your sins and made your heart a place where Christ could dwell? Have you ever been a little child, frightened and crying in a dark world of fear and sin and then felt the strong arms of our Father God enclose you and heard Jesus say: "It is I; be not afraid?" Have you not longed to have a better understanding of what happened back yonder in the old home, the old church, or in the schoolhouse or brush arbor, when a strange and blessed hope came into your heart, God's hope effectuated in you, and your condition before God was changed, and joy kept your heart in peace? Have you not meditated on a land beyond where the stars twinkle and wanted to know how and who they are that dwell in the home over there? Only the Holy Spirit can clarify and climax these visions into reality of personal knowledge in our souls even before we pass through the portals.

The hope of His Calling! Surely it must mean that we have the joyful task of trying to be like Him now, and the assurance that we shall be perfectly like Him when the day dawns and the shadows flee away; that we shall try to please Him in every thought, sentiment and act of life; that we are dedicated to the purpose of getting His work done among men; that we shall share the victory with our great Leader and Lover when He shall make us more than conquerors. The hope of His calling predicates life out of death, joy out of sorrow, sonship out of orphanhood, salvation from shame, vindication from accusation, glorification instead of humiliation, and a crown of life instead of a cross.

> "Enemies no more shall trouble,
> All thy wrongs shall be redressed;
> For thy shame thou shalt have double,
> In thy Maker's favor blessed."

The Glory of His Inheritance in the Saints

Paul never loses sight of the main point in this book, which is the glory of God through His inheritance in the saints. God, not man, is the chief actor and object of praise and adoration. Man's salvation must result in the highest eternal praise unto Him. He chose us in Christ before the founding of the world that we should be holy and blameless *before Him*. He ordained us unto sonship in Christ unto *Himself*. This was "according to the good pleasure of his will," and "unto the praise of the glory of His grace with which He graced us in the Beloved," in whom we have redemption *"according to the riches of His grace*, which He caused to abound unto us, having made known to us the *mystery of His will*, according to *His good pleasure*." The whole letter is God-centered. Much modern preaching is man-centered, hence powerless to save. That we may know the riches of the glory of His inheritance in the saints is one of the great revelations the Spirit makes to believers.

In our right spiritual mind we know that God is everything to us and for us, but we have not thought much about what we mean to Him—how He can be grieved by our sin, how His name may be reproached by our bad conduct, how His cause may be honored and promoted by loyal behavior and sacrificial service. To think and speak of what we mean to God is too high for us.

It seems to conflict with due sense of humility. The parent's love for the child and pride in the child is the way we must view it to understand this part of the prayer. The father will give everything including his life for his child. His hope is in his children. His honor and good name in the community are affected by his children. No praise is so sweet in his ears as praise of his sons and daughters; and no failure so fatal as the failure of his children. What is a successful battle to David when Absalom is gone while in rebellion against his father?

God's people are His portion. He is always thinking and working for them. His glory is in forgiving sin; in making enemies His friends; in making good men out of bad men; in showing mercy to those who deserve no mercy; in confounding angels and demons by conquering a truant world and causing it willingly to do His holy will. When the future shall be unveiled and the redeemed shall stand before God in the perfect righteousness of Christ all the hosts of heaven will be astonished and give glory to God for His righteousness that endureth forever. Only the Holy Spirit can make these precious things real and regnant in our spirits both here and hereafter.

"The Measure of Immeasurable Power"

Maclaren happily calls the third and climacteric petition of the apostle's prayer "The Measure of Immeasurable Power." "That ye may know the exceeding greatness of His power toward us who believe" is Paul's last request. He said: "The exceeding greatness of His power" but does not tell us what it exceeds. His word means "thrown-far-beyond" greatness of His power. That is greatness far beyond supreme greatness. That is omnipotence plus, or infinity outdoing itself, so to speak. When Paul thinks of himself he is "less than the least" of all saints—a comparison of a superlative. When he thinks of God's power toward believers He is far greater than His greatness, a comparison of infinity— not very good grammar, perhaps, but a marvelous way of telling what God can do for His people.

Yet there is a measure of this power. It is "according to the working of the conquering power of His mighty strength which He wrought in Christ when He raised Him from the dead." The two words "conquering power" and "mighty strength" are more or less synonymous although scholars say that the first is more "outward" and the second more "inward" in meaning, but as Maclaren says: "We need simply say that the gathering together of words so nearly co-extensive in their meaning is witness to the effort to condense the infinite within the bounds of human tongue, to speak the unspeakable; and that these reiterated expressions, like the blows of the billows that succeed one another on the beach, are hints of the force of the infinite ocean that lies behind."

This is the same power—not like unto it but the same power—that God wrought in the body of Christ when He raised Him from the tomb. If that does not add dignity and glory and certainty and finality to the work of God in believers nothing can do so. The Lord's body was dead as Lazarus was dead after four days in the tomb, but three days after Jesus was buried He astonished and overwhelmed the disciples by appearing alive in the midst of them. In the next chapter Paul tells us that the Christians had been dead in trespasses and sins—just as dead spiritually as Christ was dead physically—"But God, being rich in mercy, on account of His great love wherewith He loved us even when we were dead in trespasses made us alive together with Christ, and raised us up together (with Christ) and set us down together in the heavenly places in Christ Jesus." It is just as easy for God to make men alive from sin and dead works, and sanctify and perfect them in His heavenly kingdom, as it was for Him to raise Christ from the grave and exalt Him to His right hand on high. It is also just as difficult, if anything could be difficult for God, for the same power that wrought in Christ works in the believer.

Here is great assurance and certainty for the believer, for as we are one with Christ through the new birth into divine life we shall share with Him in the resurrection. "But each in his own order: Christ the first fruits; then they that are Christ's at His coming."

Not only is this sure destiny in Christ our possession but we can come to know it. You will not know it as you know a problem in arithmetic or in geometry. It is not subject to demonstration on a blackboard or in logical formulæ. But it is better knowledge than that. It is knowledge of experience wrought by the Holy Spirit. Christian assurance is based on three unimpeachable witnesses. They are the word of God, the testimony of an enlightened conscience, and the witness of the Holy Spirit. We know whether we are walking orderly before God. We know that we have passed out of death into life because we love God's people. We know that he that believeth on the Son hath everlasting life. And we know that the Spirit beareth witness with our spirit that we are children of God.

There is no limit to what God can do for His believing people. He can do nothing spiritually for those who stubbornly refuse to believe on Him through Christ. He gives them temporal blessings. He gives them rain and sunshine, health and fruitful seasons and abundant crops, filling their hearts with food and gladness. But the gates of mercy and salvation are barred against those who reject the Lord Jesus. "Ye would not come unto me that ye might have life" is the sad announcement of doom for disobedient men. God raised Jesus from the dead and set Him at His own right hand in the heavenly places. He gave Him a name which is above every name that has been named in this world or shall be named in the coming age. He put all things, the totality of things, animate and inanimate, whether men, angels, or demons, or powers, principalities, rulerships, and lordships of the whole universe, under His feet and gave Him, who has this universal dominion, as head of the church which is His body the fulness of Him who is filling all in all. The God of all righteousness and mercy will not redeem the Head from the grave and leave his body under dominion of death. He will not own and honor the tree and reject the branches. Our destiny is linked with His, for He is our hope, "which hope we have as an anchor of the soul both sure and steadfast and entering into that which is within the veil, whither as a forerunner Jesus entered for us, having become a high priest forever after the order of Melchizedek."

V

GRACE RAISES THE DEAD

Ephesians 2:1-7

Belshazzar's feast with a thousand of his lords, when they drank intoxicants from golden vessels which his father had stolen from the temple in Jerusalem, was not the greatest repast ever prepared, although it turned out so disastrous for him and his kingdom. Stalin's birthday party, with thirty-two alcoholic toasts, when he and his diplomats drank water from their vodka bottles, and shrewdly gave other diplomats real vodka was a hilarious occasion, but it was not the greatest feast of history.

During one of His visits to Bethany some friends of Jesus made for Him a more important feast than those just mentioned. The Bethany feast was unmatched since the world began, and can never be duplicated until this world comes to an end. One honored guest at Bethany was Lazarus whom the Lord had raised from the dead. The people at that feast knew Lazarus; they had been reared with him; they visited him in his sickness; they helped to bury his body; they mourned his death; they had seen and heard Jesus call him back to life. No wonder "the common people therefore of the Jews learned that He was there, and came not for Jesus' sake only, but that they might see Lazarus also whom He had raised from the dead."

One sister of the risen man cooked and served the feast with meticulous care and culinary skill. More sensational was the fact that another sister disturbed the decorum of the guests by breaking a valuable cruise and pouring precious ointment on the Saviour's head and feet and by dropping on her knees and wiping His feet with the flowing tresses of her rich brown hair. These things and, above all, the presence of Him who raised and restored Lazarus to the family made this feast absolutely unique and incomparable. And yet, what Jesus did for Lazarus was not a whit more wonderful than what God did for these Ephesians of whom Paul writes.

A Look at the Context

Let us look at these verses in the order in which the apostle wrote them. He did not use his main verb until he came down to our fifth verse. There are some subordinate sentences with verbs and participles, but the main verb, translated "quickened," or "made alive" is in the fifth verse.

Here is Paul's order: "And you too being dead in your trespasses and sins in which formerly ye walked according to the course of this world, according to the ruler of the power of the air, of the spirit which is now working in the sons of disobedience; among whom also we all lived (had our manner of life) formerly in the lusts of our flesh, doing the wishes of the flesh and of the thoughts and were by nature children of wrath just as also the rest; but God being rich in mercy, on account of His great love wherewith He loved us, even *when we were dead* in trespasses made us alive (his main verb) together with the Christ (whom He brought from the dead) and raised us up together with (the Christ) and seated (enthroned) us in the heavenly places in Christ Jesus, in order to show in the ages which are coming the exceeding riches of His grace in His kindness upon us in Christ Jesus."

The King James Version is correct, one thinks, in translating "dead *in* your trespasses and sins," not "by your trespasses and sins," as the Revised renders it. Men are not spiritually dead *because* they sin. They sin because they are already spiritually dead. They are born with a sinful nature. Adam sinned and brought death into the world and all our woe. "The wicked are estranged from the womb; they go astray as soon as they be born speaking lies" (Psa. 51:5). Paul says: "Therefore as through one man sin entered into the world, and death through sin; and so death passed unto all men, for that all sinned" (Rom. 5:12). The plain meaning here is that all became sinners through Adam's transgression—all sinned in Adam. He does not say: "For that all have sinned," but: "For that all sinned," using an aorist tense which refers to one act as a whole.

Some may say: "Why be so meticulous about the translation of a preposition?" There is good reason here, because a fundamental principle about the nature of men is involved. The teaching which tells us that men are born in a sinless state, and are therefore in a saved state until they personally sin and fall is not taught in the New Testament. We are born in sin and must be born again in order to be saved. "He that believeth not is condemned already because he has not believed in the name of the only begotten Son of God" (John 3:18). Paul here in Ephesians used a Locative Case "*in* trespasses and sins," showing where we were dead, not an instrumental case showing how we became dead. Dr. A. T. Robertson, great Greek expert, supports that rendering of the passage.

The apostle's word for trespasses has the root idea of

a "fall," like Adam's transgression, by the way. Man fell from the high estate of innocence in which God created him. The other word here, translated "sin," means "missing the mark," not hitting the bull's eye, as we say. "All have sinned, and fall short of the glory of God." How tragically man has failed and how helpless he is to recover himself apart from God's grace.

Being dead in sins we walked in them formerly, "according to the course of this world, according to the ruler of the power of the air, of the spirit that is now working in the sons of disobedience." "Walk" means conduct, behavior. A man's walk is one of the most characteristic things about him. You can recognize a person by his walk as far as you can see him. In sin we were dominated by the course of the world, by the age and ideals of a sinful society; were subject to the vice, corruption, indulgence, and ideologies of forces alien from God.

The power and authority of evil who is Satan, with his demonic spirits, has his dominion in the air; and the evil spirit, the world spirit, the Zeitgeist through which he controls godless men, is the one who is now working in the sons of disobedience. If it does not refer to Satan directly, it is the spirit of defiance which he inspires in godless men. "Sons of disobedience" are not simply unbelievers but those who are hardened, obstinate, defiant opposers of God.

A Terrifying Picture

The good author does not stop with expressing the sins and disobedience of the Gentiles but includes himself and all others—"among whom also we *all* lived in the lusts of our flesh, doing the wishes of the flesh and of the thoughts." So then, the Jew is just as sinful and guilty before God as is the Gentile in his carnal indulgencies.

In the King James Version, the word for lived is translated "conversation." That was a good translation in 1611 (the date of the King James Version) because then "conversation" meant "manner of life," "behavior," "citizenship." But through the years it has lost most of its meaning and now refers only to speech. "Our conversation is in heaven" means our citizenship is in heaven. It is well to remember that in the King James Version "conversation" *never* means speech or talk, but always "lived," "manner of life," "behavior," "citizenship." We all lived in our trespasses and sins, among sons of disobedience who were defiant of God. We did the wishes of the flesh and the thoughts and followed the vicious and vagrant practices of the unregenerate mind. We all, Jews and Gentiles, were by nature, or birth, children of wrath, under the wrath of God.

That is as dark a picture, as deadly a denunciation as ever was made of man's condition. It spreads a cloud as dark as midnight over his past and leaves not one glimmering star of hope for his future so far as his power to help himself is concerned. Had Paul stopped here he would have pronounced the funeral dirge of all mankind. But he was never a pessimist. He was a realist as to man's sin, but after painting the background black as ink, he enjoyed flashing on the light that it might be the more glorious in brightness. When we are oppressed by the darkness, and smothered by gloom and ready to despair and die without hope, he shouts

But God!

Now the whole world is changed and all races may pluck up courage. "But God" and the winter night of the world is passed and Spring has come to gladden and bless. "But God" and graveyards are turned into cemeteries, sleeping places of the just whose bodies await the triumphant return of their Lord. "But God" and the young mother, with clinging children, who buries her husband can return to her desolate home and take up life again in the strength of Him who has promised to be a husband to the widow and a Father to the fatherless. When his mother was ill a boy about fifteen years of age galloped a horse through deep darkness four miles to town for the doctor. The horrible thought seized him: "Suppose mother should die," and he was appalled and terrified almost to madness. "But God" and faith revived and fortitude sprang up and kept the heart in submission to Him who restored the loved one.

Hitler rose to conquer the world and, with his gas chambers came to be the most brutal murderer of all time up to his day. At Wilhelm Strasse and Unter den Linden I saw him as he was on his way to the Reich to make his speech after he proclaimed himself President. The Brown Shirts heiled him by the thousands, and it was evident that the world was in for trouble—"But God" and almost eleven years to a day from that hour he died with his concubine in the basement room of the chancelry whence he started on his spectacular ride to the Capitol.

Mussolini, a man of considerable culture and brains, who should have known better, proclaimed himself as the rebuilder of the ancient Roman Empire, but, with his mistress-companion in sin, came to his just doom, and "*sic semper tyrannis*" was written again on the minds of free men. Now Stalin, (now deceased) and Molotov, and Gromyko, and Malik, and Malenkov and all their spawn strut across the stage rattling their sabers and boasting of atomic bombs, exuding lies from every pore of their skin "but God" whom they deny and defy shall have them in derision. Many good people tremble with fear and hesitate between duty and destiny, forgetting that God is still on His throne and has no purpose to abdicate in the interest of mendacious would-be world conquerors.

The Communists have driven the missionaries out of China. They control the physical sources of information. But doors that will not open to the touch of good will may be blasted and broken with "a rod of iron" and dashed "in pieces like a potter's vessel."

A Russian officer said to Dr. Schaufler: "My imperial master, the Czar, will never allow Jesus Christ to plant His kingdom or set His foot in Turkey." The missionary straightened himself to full height and replied: "My imperial Master Jesus Christ will never ask the Czar of Russia where He may set His foot and establish His kingdom." But God being rich in mercy and unlimited in power will overrule and defeat the wrath of men and make it to praise Him.

"But God, being rich in mercy on account of His great love wherewith He loved us." How wonderful, how personal, how amazing that He loved us. The writer humbly claims a place in that "us" and asks the reader to stand by his side as a beneficiary of the same unspeakable bounty which is infinite and divine.

Made Us Alive

"But God being rich in mercy on account of His great love wherewith He loved us, *even when we were dead* in trespasses made us alive together with Christ." But what can God do for dead men, as dead as the bones Ezekiel saw in the valley? He can make them live, for

He is a plutocrat but His rule consists in riches of mercy and not in corruption of material things. His mercy is not an acquisition, not a temporary mood which He may exercise on occasion. It is His being, His nature, His very life, His unchangeable self which is forever flowing out to reach and to quicken and to save those who are dead in sin. "But God" and a world as dark as a Mamertine prison, and dead as a valley of dry bones is alive and light as the sun at noon.

He made us alive by resurrection power. In the preceding chapter we learned that the same power which God wrought in Christ in raising Him from the dead is working in believers in making them alive with Christ. This same power operates in dead souls to make them alive and will operate in dead bodies of believers to quicken them from the dead. When Christ died on the cross, He died for our sins. When we believe in Him we die to our sins and they shall not have further dominion over us. When He was raised from the dead He was raised for us, and we shall be raised at the last day to be with Him forever in glory. Being rich in mercy God not only made us alive together with Christ but

Raised Us Together with Christ

He raised us from spiritual death and we are now in the risen spiritual life with Christ, away from sin's dominion as He is in the risen life away from the grave to live forever. He passed out of the state of death of the body. We have passed out of the state of death of the soul and spirit. He is on the victory side of the grave physically. We are on the victory side spiritually. The Romans talked about Cisalpine Gaul and Transalpine Gaul. "This side of the Alps and yonder side of the

Alps." On this side there were hard climbing, narrow passes, deep snows, and biting winter. On the yonder side were broad planes, blooming flowers, and the voice of birds and children at play. Christ passed out of the state of physical death and is now with the Father in glory. Therefore our bodies shall pass out of the state of physical death and ascend to Him and His glory with the Father.

Three Great Acts of Grace

Some interpreters have not caught the meaning of Paul here. They think that "raised us up together" refers to blessings of Christian fellowship, that is "raised up together" with one another here in Christian life and activity. That is a blessed experience of believers but Paul is saying something much greater than that here. The Greek text doubtless means "raised us up together with Christ." The apostle uses three compound words all with the preposition "sun," which means "with," "association with," "together," to "be present with." Paul says: "He made us alive together with Christ, He raised us up (together with) Christ, and seated, (enthroned) us together in Christ." It is true that he does not use "Christ" in the second clause but he does continue the preposition "sun"; and the connection is so close and the construction so identical that the implication is irresistible, the conclusion inescapable; that all three "togethers" refer to Christ and not to the Christian brotherhood. He has made us alive together with Christ that we may live with Him, have fellowship with Him, represent Him to others. This life and fellowship with Him will go on here and forever.

The good apostle goes on with his victory song: "And

made us sit together in the heavenly places in Christ Jesus." That expression connotes all that Christ can be to us and all we can be to Him in mutual confidence and love both now and through eternity. It means complete surrender of the believer's will and purpose in adoring obedience to the Lord, and all His atoning and high priestly ministrations bestowed upon the believer through time and through "the generations of the age of the ages." "The heavenly places" means, one believes, in addition to present fellowship with Christ, everything that heavenly fellowship can do in giving unalloyed happiness to those who pass unafraid through a troubled world; and all that grace and glory will accomplish in bestowing perfect bliss on the saints, when the shadows have passed away and that which is perfect has come. Jesus expressed the endless felicity of heaven when He said: "Many shall come from the East and from the West, and shall sit down with Abraham and Isaac, and Jacob in the Kingdom of heaven." Then he makes it closer when he says: "I will come again and receive you unto myself that where I am there ye may be also." He touches the joy with pathos when he says: "Father, I desire that they also whom Thou hast given me may be with me where I am, that they may behold my glory which Thou hast given me." Paul's great heart, filled with homesickness, confessed: "I have a desire to depart and be with Christ for it is very far better." The unbroken dreams of perfect peace, the enchanting prospects of rapturous love, and the heart-hunger homesickness of every true disciple for complete sanctification shall all be realized here in part and there in full, "in the heavenly places in Christ Jesus." We cannot exhaust the meaning or increase the beauty of this phrase. We do not have to know everything to know the love of Christ which passes knowledge. We do not have to be perfect in order to press on "if so be that we may lay hold on that for which we were laid hold on by Christ Jesus."

Grace Demonstrated in Coming Ages

In verse seven of this chapter Paul tells us why making us alive, raising us up, and seating us in the heavenly places with Christ was done; "That He might show (demonstrate) in the coming ages the exceeding, or far-surpassing riches of His grace in His kindness upon us in Christ Jesus."

God has purposed, decreed, and determined to make it plain to all coming ages that He is a God of grace and mercy. He will not be slandered and libeled in the future life as vindictive and unjust. He will make it plain as a demonstration to all ages and intelligences that His dealings with His people, and with His enemies, have been on the highest moral, ethical, and spiritual level; that there is nothing selfish, arbitrary, unkind or unreasonable in the exercise of His power, and in the justice of His judgments. He will "justify the ways of God to men" as Milton put it in his great prayer as he began Paradise Lost. The Hymn writer expressed it as follows:

"O the love that drew salvation's plan,
O the grace that brought it down to man,
O the mighty gulf that God did span at Calvary.
Mercy there was great and grace was free,
Pardon there was multiplied to me.
There my burdened soul found liberty at Calvary."

Paul here, as elsewhere, never turns from his purpose to set forth the grace of God and the glory of God through the manifestation of that grace to men. "That He might show to the coming ages the far-surpassing riches of His grace." The most wonderful thing in the universe is that God loves fallen men; and that He is active, aggressive in making known the incomparable riches of His provision for them. He shows and showers the surpassing riches of His grace in His kindness "upon us." Paul says that the medium through which He bestows it is "in Christ Jesus." The object or purpose of it is to enhance, and demonstrate and publicize in all coming ages His matchless grace, His superlative kindness upon His people in the redemptive sacrifice of our Lord. "All the races of mankind and all future ages are embraced in the redeeming purpose and are to share in its boundless wealth. Nor are the ages past excluded from its operations. God afore prepared the good works in which He summons us to walk. The highway of the new life has been in building since time began"—The Ex. Bible. The only thing that can prevent this rich heritage is the rejection of the Redeemer.

Note the wealth of the provision. It is riches. It is surpassing riches. It is surpassing riches of His grace. It is riches of His grace mutiplied in superlative kindness. The demonstration of the surpassing riches of His grace is bestowed on us poor mortals in life, and death, and eternity.

Paul expresses a blessed redundancy of it for which he is not ashamed. "Grace be to you from God our Father and the Lord Jesus Christ." "Who blessed us with every spiritual blessing in the heavenly places in Christ." "According as He chose us in Him before the foundation of the world." "The adoption of sons through Jesus Christ." "Wherewith He blessed us in the Beloved." "In whom we have redemption through His blood." "Which He purposed in Him." "To sum up all things in Christ." "In Him in whom we were made a heritage." "We who first hoped in Christ." " In *whom* also ye when ye heard the word of the truth." "In whom also when ye had believed ye were sealed." "Having heard of the faith among you in the Lord Jesus." "That the God of our Lord Jesus Christ might give unto you the spirit of wisdom and revelation." "According to the working of His mighty strength which He wrought in Christ." "When He raised *Him* from the dead and set *Him* at his right hand." "And put all things under *His* feet." "And gave *Him* head over all things to the church." Some twenty-one times in the first chapter Paul refers to Christ, and fourteen times in the second, ten times in the third, fifteen in the fourth—sixty times in the first four chapters, and on to the end he goes striking this harp of melody in which his soul ever delights.

Some irreverant critics have suggested that it is glorified selfishness for God to publicize His goodness and grace to men. Many unbelieving hearts make a stumbling block even of God's efforts to save them. Is it selfishness for a mother to shower her love and bounty on her child and write her love and name on its heart? Is it selfishness for an adoring lover to fall at the feet of his loved one and devote his life and love and substance for her happiness?

The highest and most just praise that God can ever have will be that He loved His enemies, that He was kind to the unworthy, that He raised dead souls to eternal life with Himself. If men are not saved it will not be God's fault, but their own wilfulness. All the coming ages will be informed of the exceeding riches of His grace in His kindness upon us in Christ Jesus.

The bounty is enough for all who will have it. There is no excuse for poverty in the midst of riches untold.

The water of life can slake every thirst. The Father's table will feed all who will come to it through His grace in Christ Jesus. The Father's home is large enough for all who become His children through faith in His Son.

One has seen the gospel convict and conquer an infidel school teacher, who was graduated at the University of Chicago, and make of him a humble follower of the Lord. One has seen the gospel lift up and save fallen women and send them forth as ministers of mercy and evangels of the good news of salvation. One has known tipplers to turn from their bottles, and gamblers to discard their cards and devote themselves to the Galilean because of the knowledge of His truth.

God will have something to tell the angels in that day of revelation about the exceeding riches of His grace, and what it has meant to believers in Christ. Every mouth shall be stopped and every tongue shall confess that Christ is Lord to the glory of God the Father.

The universal recognition of the magnitude of God's grace and kindness to His people is the purpose and goal of His plan, and the motivation of His activities. His very purpose in working these marvels in the life of His people is to display before all races, peoples, and nations His wonderful, immeasurable, eternal, unspeakable, prevenient, amazing grace which He has provided in Christ, imparts through Christ, and forever perpetuates in Christ.

This is to be shown in coming eternal ages. The purpose of eternity is working, and converging and consummating all things and all peoples, and all powers in order to exhibit the exceeding riches of God's grace and kindness unto His people whom He has redeemed, not with silver and gold but by the precious blood of Christ.

"When we look at Christ we see the divinest thing in

God, and that is His grace. The Christ who shows us and certifies to us the grace of God must surely be more than man. Men look at Him and see it. He shows us that grace because He was full of grace and truth"— Maclaren.

> "T'was grace that taught my heart to fear,
> And grace my fears relieved,
> How precious did that grace appear
> The hour I first believed."

VI

GRACE SAVES AND SANCTIFIES

Eph. 2:8-10

When charged with the murder of Jesus and told that He had been raised from the dead and exalted to the right hand of God, the murderers of the Master were pierced through their heart and cried out: "Brethren what shall we do?"

Likewise the Philippian jailor with blanching face and quivering lips, rushed into the prison and fell down before Paul and Silas and said: "Sirs, what must I do to be saved?" When conscience revives and the sense of personal sin smites the soul like a besom of destruction men see the specter of judgment and plead for help. No words can measure the tragedy of being lost or evaluate the eternal benefit of being saved.

In this passage of Ephesians (2:8-10), Paul tells how men must be saved; then show faith by works.

There are many discordant, jarring voices about how people can be saved. But after all there are only two branches of teaching concerning salvation. One teaches that salvation comes through works, the other teaches that salvation is by grace. All dogmas and discussions about how men are saved can be reduced to one of these. All the schemes that man has devised for his salvation are based on man's work or merit. God's plan for saving us roots itself deep in His eternal and benevolent purpose of grace. "For by grace have ye been saved through faith, and that not of yourselves, it is the gift of God, not of works, that no one should glory" (Eph. 2:8).

Notice that statement. First, it is by grace, which means the undeserved favor of God. Second, "Ye have been saved," which is a perfect passive tense Indic. mood, indicating the thing has been done in past time and the act has resulted in a continued state of being in present time, and will go on in the future. In other words, it is an operative fact or condition in the present about which there is no doubt, uncertainty, or apprehension concerning its continuance. Third, it is not from or out of us. Fourth, it is God's gift, with special emphasis on "God." Fifth, it is not of "works," the plural, including all works. Sixth, it is so arranged that nobody can boast of his own salvation.

It Is By Grace

Salvation is simply and gloriously by the grace of God. It does not stem from anything but the grace, unmerited favor, prevenient love, eternal benevolence of God. We get in salvation the greatest thing in the universe from God when we really *deserve* His frown in eternal condemnation.

We Do Not Deserve Salvation

The only true premise from which to argue this question is that we do not deserve to be saved. We have sinned and defied God. We are sinners by nature and have practiced sin. There was no moral requirement on God to do a thing for us. He could have let us go to hell without having any blood on His hands. The only constraint on God was His own loving disposition which inclined or conditioned Him to help the undeserving.

The reason for His action in our behalf was deep in His own heart, and not in any work or any merit found in us.

"But doesn't a man have to do something to be saved?", I hear a poor sinner say. No, not one thing in this world but to accept salvation. Salvation is a gift and what do you have to do to get a gift? Just *take* it, that is all. If a man offered to give you a nice gift he would be offended if you offered to pay for it! When God offers you Christ as salvation He won't like it if you think you can pay Him.

It All Begins With God

God's grace not only means that salvation is a gift, but also that everything about salvation *begins* with God. When we were dead God had to make us alive so we could know and understand Him. When we were blind He had to make us see. When we were lost He had to find us.

See how much God has done for us. He loved us. He gave Christ to die for us. He sent the Holy Spirit to warn and convict us. He provided the Bible to teach us. He raised up prophets to rebuke us for our wrong doing and hardness of heart. Even repentance and faith are inspired and motivated by a loving God. The Bible says that Christ was exalted to "give repentance and remission of sins unto Israel." A wicked man will not repent until the Holy Spirit convicts him of sin. He will not believe until God shows him Christ his sin bearer. "But doesn't God command men everywhere to repent?" Certainly, and "Except ye repent ye shall all likewise perish." God leads and holds us responsible for following His leadership. If God had perfected a plan of salvation and then flung it out to a world of

sinful men and said: "Take it or leave it," they all would
have left it. He had to follow up the plan by hanging
Christ on a cross, by raising Him from the dead, by
sending the Spirit to convict men of sin, righteousness,
and judgment.

Grace Is Love On a Quest

Grace is much more than a negative force. Grace
is active, diligent, positive, wideawake benevolence seeking to show kindness on all who will receive it. Grace
is love on an undying quest for those who are not lovely.
Grace is like a mother on a determined search for her
lost child; nay grace is more, grace is like a benevolent
King, hunting for a vagabond orphan in order to make
him a son of the royal family and an heir of the King's
domain.

Grace is the aggressive activity of God seeking the
sinful, loving the unlovely, helping the helpless, and saving the lost. Grace is a compassionate forgiving love as
deep as the being and life of God.

Grace thought of us and planned for us before we ever
thought of ourselves; just like a mother is thinking and
planning for the child before it is born. Grace thinks of
us, loves us and seeks us when we are in sin, just as a
mother follows a wayward child and begs him to come
home.

Grace always wants to help and never to harm us.
The purpose, the cause, the plan, the basis, yea and even
the method of our salvation find their beginning in God.
God has a great love story for everybody who will listen
to Him. a great gift for all who will receive it. One has
seen little children who were afraid of Santa Claus, because of his strangeness and unusual dress, draw back
from him, but when they were shown the lovely presents

he had the timidity was overcome and they nestled in his arms. Let it be so with God, dear lost man, for He comes only to bless and give. He is all good and no evil, all love and no hate, all mercy and no malice, all riches and no poverty, all life and no death for your soul, if you believe on His Son.

Works Cannot Save

Good works cannot save you, first because they are more evil than good; because the heart is evil and God requires perfection; second, because they cannot change your heart and make you aceptable to God; third, because they have no power to forgive sin, or justify you before God.

Works were never intended to save men, either in the Old or New Testament times. The Scripture classifies them as filthy rags when they are presented for righteousness.

God's law even, cannot save you. Paul says that the law is a "schoolmaster" to lead us to Christ. The law was given to condemn us, to show us that we are sinners, and not to justify us—"for by the law there shall no flesh be justified in His sight." Works of love, deeds of mercy are good for Christians to do, but they are the result, not the cause, of salvation. The "seven sacraments" and seven thousand more cannot forgive one sin. Neither preachers, nor priests, nor mothers, nor wives, with all their love, can purge away sin.

The ordinances of the church, baptism and the Lord's supper, good and symbolic as they are of salvation, cannot save the soul. Those who trust baptism and the Lord's Supper to forgive their sins will die and meet God unprepared.

Prayer cannot save the soul although it may help the

heart to surrender to Christ the Lord through whom alone God saves. One who lived and talked with Jesus said: "Neither is there salvation in any other, for there is none other name under heaven given among men whereby we MUST be saved."

Not of yourself, your merit; not by good works; not by conformity (which you can't fulfill) with the commandments of the law of God; not by the ordinances of the church—not by anything or everything under heaven in the nature of works can you be saved. It is the gift of God in Christ Jesus our Lord.

Through Faith

How can men make contact with the saving grace of God? Paul says that it is done through faith. Christ is God's salvation, therefore you have it or it has you, when you believe on Christ. Faith is a very simple idea, so simple indeed that it is difficult to explain it. It is trust. It is commitment, not to a proposition but to a Person. It is acceptance of Christ with the will, the heart, the conscience, the affections. It is the taking of Christ as the Master and Monitor of one's life and love; the One who is Lord of purpose and person. The New Testament offers salvation to no responsible persons except believers. To those who cried out for mercy on the day of Pentecost Peter said: "Repent ye, and let each one of you be baptized upon the name of Jesus Christ for (because of) the remission of your sins, and ye shall receive the gift of the Holy Spirit" (Acts 2:38). In this text "repent ye" agrees in number with "ye shall receive," both plural. "Let each one be baptized" is singular, indicating that each one who has repented is a subject for baptism because he has repented and his sins are forgiven. The plural in the first clause and the last clause shows that persons who repent receive the Holy Spirit. The Greek preposition (eis) here means "because of," not "in order to," although it does sometimes mean in order to. It is the same use of the preposition as that found in Matt. 10:41, 42 "*in* the name of a righteous man," and "*in* the name of a prophet," where it *must* be translated "because of." Any other rendering would destroy the sense of the passages. There are several other passages where the preposition must be translated "because of." Some competent scholars think "unto," "with reference to" is a good translation—much the same as because of.

The Philippian jailor knew from the earthquake and the open prison doors that the power of God was present. He was convicted of his ill treatment of the innocent apostles. He was conscious of his sins in the sight of God, (repentant); so rushing into the prison, stricken with terror, he fell down before Paul and Silas, then brought them out and said: "Sirs, what must I do to be saved?" "And they said believe on the Lord Jesus and thou shalt be saved and thy house." Faith would supply his need, and faith would meet the need of his house. It does not mean that *his* faith would save his household, but they could be saved in the same way that he could.

This is a wonderful scripture. It is the only place where exactly that question is asked in the Bible (Acts 16:30, 31). A jailor in great distress cries for instruction about how to be saved. The apostle Paul said: "Believe on Christ and you shall be saved." In this instance he said nothing about repentance, but the jailor was already repentant. He said nothing about keeping the law and doing good works. When the jailor believed and was saved he could be trusted to walk in righteousness. Paul said nothing about baptism as a condition of salvation. Baptism would come after the jailor was saved, as it did.

VII

GRACE UNITES ALL BELIEVERS

Chap. 2:11-22

Personal hatreds and race antagonisms are hard to cure. There is no bigotry more relentless than religious intolerance, no slavery more despicable and deadly than blind prejudice. This condition was rife between Jews and Gentiles in the time of Jesus. A feeling of superiority on the part of the one and a supreme contempt and hauteur in the mind of the other made an impossible barrier between them, "a middle wall of partition," as Paul calls it, which nothing but the grace of redemption could remove. Only the miracle of divine love could effect reconciliation, and produce brotherhood between such hostile groups. This happy consummation reminds us of the poet's words:

> "He drew a circle that shut me out,
> Heretic, rebel, a thing to flout;
> But love and I had the wit to win,
> We drew a circle that took him in."

But it is only the love of God in Christ that enables enemies to draw that circle that takes "him" in; only when both men are changed by grace can they draw the circle and then live at peace within the circle, because they are of one heart and one soul. They are of one mind and one purpose, having been reconciled by the blood of the Cross. This section of Ephesians, 2:11-22, shows how this miracle of reconciliation is brought about.

"Wherefore," in the beginning of this paragraph, applies the teaching of the preceding section to the Gentile Christians. They are admonished to remember that sometime they were Gentiles in the flesh, who are called uncircumcision by that which is called circumcision in the flesh made by hands; because "ye were at that time without (apart from) Christ, being completely alienated (it's a perfect passive participle) from the commonwealth of Israel." "Commonwealth" is the translation of a word which comes from one that means "to be a citizen." It is the root from which we get our word politics. The Greek word "polis" meaning "city" which we meet in "metropolis," mother city, is the parent word, the noun in fact, from which the other comes. Most people lived in cities then. To be a "citizen" was to live in a city. To have a commonwealth was to have a city-government. Then, a city man should be a good citizen—not always the case however. They were completely alienated from the commonwealth of Israel and strangers (those who were not citizens) from the covenants of the promise.

"Having no hope" is not only without the Christian hope, but utterly confused, without any and all hope. "Without God" is the Greek word atheist—godless, but in the original use it meant "impious, irreverent toward the gods." "But now," in verse thirteen, gives sharp contrast with "at that season." "But now in Christ Jesus you who were formerly far off are become nigh in the blood of Christ." "For He Himself is our peace," the apostle continues, "who made the both one." He uses the article to point out both Jews and Gentiles. "And broke down the middle wall of partition having abolished in His flesh the enmity, even the law of commandments contained in ordinances, that He might create in Himself of the two (the article again) one new man, so making peace." Consequently He will reconcile them both (Jew and Gentile) in one body to God through the cross, having slain the enmity by it. "In one body," here refers to their unity in one body, not to His body. He has already said above that they "are become nigh in the blood of Christ." This provision for unity in Christ, this slaying of the enmity which had separated them has prepared for the proclamation of the gospel unto both—"and having come he preached peace unto you (Gentiles) who were far off, and peace to those who were nigh" (Jews). "For through him we both have access in one Spirit to the Father." The sacrifice was for both Jews and Gentiles, the gospel message or proclamation is for both, the same access is for both, and the approach is directed, mediated, by the one Spirit. "Consequently now therefore ye are no longer strangers or sojourners but rather ye are fellow citizens with the saints and the household of God." The state of the Gentiles is so changed that they are not just visitors, "paying guests" as landladies euphemistically call their boarders. They are not sojourners or fly-by-night travelers but citizens of the commonwealth and members of the household. They are not boarders, not sojourners, but members of the household and heirs of all the Father's wealth. That is the difference between a citizen and a sojourner, between a child and a servant, between being an alien and dwelling as a son in the father's house.

No wonder Paul admonishes the Gentiles to remember their former estate. It is not good to forget the mortar in which we were brayed. Certainly we should remember it in contrast with better conditions and greater blessings of the present.

Great disadvantage has been alleged against the Gentiles. They were opprobriously dubbed "the uncircumcision" who had no sign in the flesh that God had called or claimed them as his own. Uncircumcision was an epithet as disreputable as "Samaritans" or "untouchables." They were thus stigmatized by those who in a lordly fashion called themselves "the circumcision." Paul however, deflates the "Jews of their boasting when he terms it "circumcision in the flesh made with hands," and not spiritual separation of heart and life from the world unto God.

Hark back to "Ye were afar off but now ye have become nigh in the blood of Christ." How the blood of Christ despises and surmounts all physical handicaps and turns them to the advantage of the under-privileged! Ye were without peace but now Christ Himself, in His divine person as well as in His atoning mediatorial work, is your peace. Ye *were* separated from the holy place by an impassable partition wall, but Christ has demolished that in his body. That wall caused the bitterest hatred, enmity itself. The law of commandments written in ordinances which the Jews constantly extolled, and as constantly broke, stood as a barrier between them. This, Christ has forever abolished in His death, that He might create both in Himself one new man and so make peace. This ancient enmity which has so long divided them from their human brothers, was slain when He died on the cross, that they both might die unto themselves and become one new man in him. There was no peace for those afar off or for those who were nigh until He came in His blood and made peace to the aliens and peace to the household of Israel. Not alone what the Lord did but His own blessed person and Godhood, which combines the divine nature and prerogatives of God in the same person with the nature of man, stands ever between God and man as Mediator and High Priest of our salvation.

This divine one, perfect in all His nature and qualifications as Mediator, did something of indispensable value. He set about a complete reconciliation of these hostile groups of men. One group, with contemptuous superiority, gloried in their ancestry and traditions; and pompously proclaimed their own righteousness, and majored on the privilege of being the mouthpiece of God to all men, while they looked with undisguised scorn on all whose family tree did not stem from the stock of Israel. The other group were in darkest ignorance of spiritual truth; had no light and knowledge of religious history and tradition; were given to the most shameful vices and immoralities; were dead as corpses in their trespasses and sins; and lived according to the debasing standards of the age. They wore the yoke of the devil who is the god of this world and the ruler of the power of the air. The chief animation and activity of each group was their inveterate hatred and opposition to the other group. How can people of such complexities, such adverse ideals, such warring purposes, such conflicting racial sympathies ever be brought together in spirit and bound by the same hope and peace? Jesus broke down the enmity and made them into one new man by the sacrifice of Himself.

The law had been a barrier to the Gentiles and a burden on the necks of the Jews. That which had been intended for their good they had turned into their own condemnation. They had made it a wall of separation and offense between themselves and other nations instead of a means of enlightenment and instruction for all. It had produced not only a hostile feeling but the feeling had hardened into a state of enmity itself. The law was never intended to save men but only to make them know the need of a Savior. Abraham could no more be saved by it than could Paul. They had taken the shadow for the substance, the circumcision of the foreskin for the separation of the heart unto God, which circumcision signified. They had impounded the spirit of the law with a wall of ceremonies and vain formalities. When Christ died on the cross "the law of commandments" was abolished for the Christian. That does not mean that God's people are encouraged to sin. They are so re-made in Christ that they do not want to sin. When *they* are under the law of the Spirit of life in Christ Jesus they are free from the law of sin and death. Guided by the Holy Spirit they do those things contained in the perfect law of liberty. That is more nearly a perfect state than anybody can ever attain under a law of commandments. Men cannot be saved by the works of the law, neither can they be sanctified by deeds of righteousness apart from the sanctifying Spirit.

The law is a school master to lead us to Christ. Paul used the word "pedagogue" which sometimes means a "boy-leader." A father who had an obstreperous son that would not go to school would appoint one of his servants to lead the boy to school, willing or unwilling. They called that servant a "boy-leader," a pedagogue. That is our case in our disobedience. The law, with its frightful maledictions and terrible condemnation, causes us to seek forgiveness in Christ. Then the law has performed its mission. The condemnation of the law is removed not because anybody ever obeyed it perfectly, but because Christ obeyed it perfectly and filled it full. It never made a demand on Him that He did not satisfy in His life and in His substitutionary death. Because He died under the law we die to it when we believe in Him. Because He rose from the grave we rise to newness of life and love and obedience in Him. If He abolished the law, as Paul says, then we are not under law, but under grace. It is passing strange that anybody who has been redeemed by the precious blood of Christ, and delivered from the bondage of the law, should want to go back to the servitude of that old yoke of which Peter said "neither we nor our fathers were able to bear it."

What was God's purpose in abolishing "the law of commandments?" Paul gives the answer, "In order that He might create in Himself the two into one new man, so making peace." There was no other way to make peace between the warring groups, no other way to form peace in human hearts that were torn by war and hate. Sinful nature is belligerent and divisive. It is like a warden of an asylum said when asked what would happen if the patients were to get together and attack the attendants. He said: "They have not sense enough to get together." Unregenerate men have not sense enough to get together. Now that the shooting war is over the nations have not sense enough to conclude a peace. The nations must learn the way of peace by being grafted into Christ. Russia is the world's menace today because her rulers know nothing of the ethics of Jesus, nothing of the golden rule, nothing of the doctrine of "in honor preferring one another." The person and work of the Lord constitute the only basis of permanent peace in the heart and peace on earth. There can not be strife for an hour at the cross where "mercy and truth are met together; righteousness and peace have kissed each other." Oh, the nations will devastate and destroy one another forever, and men will fight and kill and perish in hell unless they meet at the cross and bury their weapons and become one new man in Christ Jesus.

What a *great costly* thing is Redemption! When the

cross was erected animosities died and brotherly love
was born. Then the message of peace could be proclaimed to all men. It is all common ground at the cross.
A story says that when Lord Wellington was kneeling
at the chancel rail to receive the Lord's supper, somebody said to a meanly dressed boy near Wellington:
"Don't crowd the Duke," to which the grim old soldier
replied: "Let him alone, we are all equal here." There
are not reservations for some of the children and a warning "Verboten" for others; no holier than thou attitudes,
no class distinctions and favoritisms in the kingdom of
grace. All are glad bond slaves of Christ and all are free
in him. The kingdom of God is the only true democracy
in the sense that all are equal in rights and privileges. The
way to the Father is a way of suffering, a "via dolorosa,"
splotched with the blood and tears of Him who carried
a cross, but it has been made safe for the feet of all who
journey to Calvary.

New Relationships

A new relationship to Christ makes a new relation to
men. One knew a man and his wife who were worthy
in moral character but not Christians. They were unknown in the town and unrecognized socially. The minister found them and brought Christ to them in the home.
They joined the church and began a faithful Christian
life, and lo, soon they were received in the best homes
and were bearing an honorable part in teaching and in
other church activities. The Lord took them from ob-
scurity and set them in a large place of influence. Christ
was not only the salvation of their souls but the giver of
social contacts and pleasures and friendships which were
impossible apart from the kingdom of God. Give the

gospel a chance and it will make everybody into Somebody. After all, the only family tree that has no bad limbs is the tree of the cross. The highest born are children of the "First born from the dead," who is the "effulgence of the Father's glory and the very image of his substance." The Gentiles in Christ have just as good birth certificate as do the Jews. Their place at the table is secure for they are children in their Father's house. Their inheritance is "incorruptible, and undefiled and fadeth not away," and is "reserved in heaven for you who are guarded by the power of God through faith unto a salvation which is ready to be revealed in the last time."

Rights and Privileges

To be a citizen means to have rights, immunities, privileges and duties. To be a fellow citizen with the saints is to enjoy life fellowship with the holiest and highest society known to earth and heaven; while to be the household of God is to dwell in the Father's house both now and forever more. Their footing is not ground of shifting sand or miry clay. Their feet have been placed on a rock and their goings have been established. "You have been built upon the foundation which was laid by the apostles and prophets, who preached Christ to you, Jesus Christ Himself being the chief cornerstone." One used to think that text meant that the apostles and prophets were a part of the foundation. Not so, Christ is the whole foundation. "Other foundation can no man lay than that which is laid which is Jesus Christ." The chief cornerstone" is by a figure of speech put for the whole. It is the foundation of apostles and prophets only in the sense that they laid it by the preaching of the gospel. Nobody shares the honor of being the foundation with

Christ; and nobody can add one ounce of strength to it except by proclaiming Him as the foundation on which all men must stand.

It is mathematically true that adding to or taking from infinity does not change its quantity in the least. The wiseacres who would attenuate Christ to the size of a man do not affect Him a particle. They only blight and damn themselves. "Everyone therefore that heareth these words of mine and doeth them, shall be likened unto a wise man who built his house on the rock; and the rain descended and the floods came and the winds blew, and beat upon that house, and it fell not, for it was founded upon the rock." But oh, the foolish man who built on the sand, and the complete ruin that followed!

"In whom," the writer goes on in verse twenty-two, "every building which is being fitly joined together is growing into a holy temple in the Lord." "Fitly joined together" is expressed by a present participle in Paul's language, showing that the work is in process, not completed yet. There is great difficulty in this passage, first as to whether we should translate it "every building" or "the whole building," as the King James Version renders it. "The whole building" seems to suit the context better. "Every building" seems to destroy the unity of the Gentiles and Jews which the paragraph is arguing. But "every building" has the grammatical advantage. The rule is that wherever the Greek word "pasa" "all" is used with a noun that does not have the definite article you *must* translate it "every." Where the noun has the article you *must* translate it "all" or "the whole." In this case the noun is anarthrous, therefore the translation is "every building"

Now if we translate this passage: "In whom every building which is being fitly joined together is growing

into an holy temple in the Lord," what is the meaning of
"every building?" Paul is, no doubt, carrying out the
figure of speech he has used before in his reference to
"foundation," and "household of God." But to what
does he refer, to each particular church, or to each particular believer? Is he speaking of the sanctification of
each Christian or of each congregation or church of
believers which is growing in grace and becoming a
holy temple of the Lord? If it refers to a particular
church, which would imply a plurality of churches, then
they *must* be many churches of the same faith. Otherwise the unity of which he speaks could not be realized.
He could not mean there are many buildings (churches)
of different kinds without violating the whole context
which argues for unity of Gentiles and Jews in Christ.
When we remember that Ephesians is most probably a
circular letter, written to all the churches of the Lychus
river valley, and not a letter addressed specifically to
the church of Ephesus ("in Ephesus" 1:1 is not in the
best manuscripts) may not, indeed does not, "every
building" refer to any one of those churches or to all
of them separately considered, and to all Christ's local churches in all ages? With that interpretation "every
building" will mean any one of those churches in
the Lychus river valley, and every New Testament
church which is in the process of being fitly joined
together which is growing into a holy temple of the
Lord. Every church of believers is the Church of
God. "Fitly framed together" means the joints properly
joined, integrated and framed so as to be harmonious and
natural in use and functioning. But many churches are
out of joint. Their hinges grate, their joints are swollen
and sore with arthritis.

Every church is a totality, an entity, an individual in

its own right and organism. It is divinely endowed with freedom, autonomy, self-control without interference from any source but the Lord, the head of the church. But it is not a law unto itself. It is under orders from its head. It may not take liberty with the principles as laid down in the guide book, the New Testament. The church, every church, is charged with important duties. Free under Christ in its own government it is not free to dally and loiter in matters of duty, or to wait for other churches to perform their obligations before it moves forward in Christ's work. It may and should cooperate with other churches in missionary and benevolent work but must not wait for laggards when souls are dying and Christ is saying "Go." It is the duty of every church, if there were no other one, to evangelize the whole world. That is the commission the Jerusalem church received.

The apostle is saying here that each church, founded on Christ, and joined in harmonious fellowship and service and sanctification of the Spirit and belief of the truth, constitutes a spiritual unity as indissoluble as a great temple with every stone bound hard and fast to every other stone. A church must constantly grow by the addition of living stones to the temple, and by the increase, enrichment, and adornment of all the member stones of the building.

A New Testament church is not a part of any other organization and cannot become a constituent part of any other body without surrendering its essential character. It may cooperate with other bodies in its own freedom but cannot be compounded with any other church, club, state organization, or ecclesiasticism. The New Testament knows no such thing as many churches being bound together into an ecclesiastical system and being ruled over by the authority of men. The church is to operate in all the world, and preach the gospel to all nations, but a union of many churches into an ecclesiastical organization which rules over dioceses and domains is utterly foreign to New Testament teaching. Christ is the head of the church, every church, and He never delegates His authority to popes, priests, prelates, patriarchs, presbyteries or to bishops (scriptural or unscriptural kind), or even to deacons valuable and excellent as they may be. Christ lives in all the members if they are living stones and empowers and authorizes them to carry on in their corporate capacity the business of the Lord. The church itself cannot surrender its own freedom with which the Lord has endowed it. It can act through committees but must not delegate the authority Christ has delegated to it. Unified in Christ the church is not an organization but a living organism growing into maturity, or full grown stature in the Lord. Never territorial in its constitution its field is the world with a mission and commission to bring all world territory into submission to Christ. Never dominated by other churches it should cooperate with them in their purpose to make Christ supreme, and should count itself subservient to the needs and fellowship of all men in the Lord.

Paul carries the thought on to the glorious climax, the eternal, spiritual consummation of the life of the church, when he says: "In whom also ye are being builded together for a habitation of God in the Spirit." When he spoke of their salvation he used a past perfect tense which brings a completed passed action into a present state of fact. See 2:8 "by grace have ye been saved." But now when he speaks of their sanctification, of their being builded together for a habitation of God in the Spirit," he uses a present tense to set forth the process of their growth in unity and completeness. You

are not only being built into a holy temple, the apostle
would say, but you are being builded together for God's
present and eternal habitation. The growth that is going
on in the lives of the members and the increasing unity
of the whole body of believers in all the churches of
Christ are perfecting the whole body as a fit dwelling
place of God in His Holy Spirit. When all the redeemed
are glorified the general assembly and church of the
First Born will have come to pass. In this God's fulness
will dwell forever.

VIII

UNSEARCHABLE RICHES OF GRACE

Eph. 3:1-13

It is a good thing, sometimes, for preachers to be put in jail. Had Bunyan not gone to jail we should not have had The Pilgrim's Progress. Without the imprisonment of John Weatherford and others Virginia Baptists would have been deprived of the most illustrious Chapter of their history. Polycarp, John Huss, and Hubmeyer, at the fiery stake, kindled a light which has never flickered or failed. The imprisonment of Paul and Silas at Philippi, with their feet fast in the stocks, resulted in the jailor's salvation, which brought prestige to Christianity.

This "citizen of no mean city" was big enough to go to jail without boasting as a martyr and proclaiming himself a hero or suffering from an inferiority complex. He starts the paragraph with: "For this cause I Paul the prisoner of Christ Jesus in behalf of you the Gentiles" —then goes on a long detour which lasts through verse thirteen. However he is not parading himself as "the prisoner" by way of pre-eminence. "The article here expresses simply the character in which he appears or the class to which he belongs, not his pre-eminence among the Lord's prisoners as if he were the prisoner par excellence" (Ex. G.T.). He was in jail for the Gentiles because he was the apostle to the Gentiles and was now in prison for preaching the gospel.

In beginning his digression he writes: "If so be that

ye did hear of the dispensation of the grace of God which was given me to you-ward," etc. "If" here does not express doubt or uncertainty. It is a form of condition in the language Paul was using which expects an affirmative answer. It does not assert that the thing is true, but treats it as true, takes it hypothetically as a fact. You might well translate his clause "If indeed ye heard as I assume ye did, of the dispensation of the grace of God which was given to me to you-ward." "You-ward," as the King James and the American Standard versions both read, is an excellent rendering of Paul's phrase. He received the dispensation (or plan, or arrangement) of the grace of God for them. It was directed toward them in its ethical purpose.

In verse three he claims the dignity and authority of a revelation which was made to him about what he calls "the mystery." It was not evolved from his "inner consciousness." A process of reasoning did not discover it. Neither did man's wisdom make it known. It was revealed (uncovered the Greek word means) to him when the Lord appeared to him on the Damascus road and Ananias came and interpreted to him his strange experience, and gave him his commission.

We meet with an interesting use of the word "mystery" here. Mystery as Paul used it does not mean something which cannot be understood, or something difficult to be understood, but something that must be revealed in order to be understood. He says: "Ye have heard of the dispensation of the grace of God which was given to me for you, how that according to revelation there was made known to me the mystery, even as I wrote before in a few words (Chap. 2:11-20) to the end that ye may be able when ye read, to know my insight in the mystery of Christ, which in former generations was not made known to the sons of men as it has now been revealed to His holy apostles and prophets in the Spirit, namely, that the Gentiles are fellow-heirs and fellow-body members and fellow-partakers of the promise in Christ Jesus through the gospel."

Note some great things here. First, the mystery of Christ was a revelation to him. Second, they would recognize his insight into the mystery. Every generation that has studied him has recognized his insight. Moreover, every preacher has an insight in the mystery of Christ. If not, his commission is bogus, false. Every preacher must be tested, is tested by his power to understand and interpret Christ to the people. In the third place, the mystery he speaks of was not made known to former generations as it has now been revealed to the apostles and prophets. These were New Testament apostles and prophets. A prophet may be a foreteller, but is chiefly a forthteller. As intercessor, he speaks to God for men, as prophet he speaks to men for God. A fourth thing of supreme importance is that it has been revealed by and in the Holy Spirit. Both ideas of "by" and "in" the Spirit seem to be here. He is the agent by whom the revelation came, which men never could have known but for Him, and He is the person and power in whom the revelation consists.

Paul holds in abeyance the definition of the mystery until the sixth verse is reached, and here it is: "That the Gentiles are fellow-members of the body and fellow-partakers of the promise in Christ Jesus through the gospel." These privileges are granted to the Gentiles the same as to Jews. It was always God's eternal plan that the Gentiles should be brought into the covenant of grace. They are as truly heirs of God as are the Jews; they are just as truly members of His body. To put it otherwise, the fact that the grace of God is for all races, nations, and people of this world is a revelation from God. Nobody ever knew that until God revealed it in Christ, and many belated, self-centered souls have not yet understood the revelation. Foreign missions, home missions, racial missions, worldwide missions were all included in the eternal purpose of God. To reject this is to fight against God's eternal plan and to ignore the universal redemptive purpose of Christ in His sufferings. Of this gospel Paul says that he became a servant according to the gift of the grace of God which was given to him according to the working of His power.

At this point the preacher gives an estimate, a character sketch of himself. It is interesting to know what people say about themselves. *Who's Who in America*, is a rather famous publication made up of what men and women have written about themselves. One believes that the biographees in that publication have correctly chronicled their life activities, but you will not find the self-depreciatory remarks there which we read in Ephesians 3:8.

This greatest of all preachers who wrote Ephesians said: "I am less than the least of all saints." He chose a very little used Greek word which is all but ungrammatical and expresses a contradiction in terms, "less than the least" to tell us how insignificant he was. A well worn story worth recalling tells how an aged, humble minister said to a youngster, who had gone into the pulpit with great self-confidence and miserably failed, and then came out in deep humiliation: "If you had gone into the pulpit in the spirit in which you came out, you might have come out with the spirit with which you went in." Paul had great confidence but it was based on God, not on himself. The greatest men are modest, almost without exception. One remembers the greatest men he has ever known as the most modest and unassuming. For the greatest devotee of Christ to take his seat on the lowest rung of the ladder of spiritual ascent ought to cast crowns of ambition, and badges of distinction into the gutter.

John Richard Green, the English historian, said: "Say of me he died learning." Thomas Jefferson in choosing his memorial never mentioned the fact that he had been President of the United States, or an ambassador to France, but said that he wrote the "Declaration," the *Virginia Statute of Religious Liberty*, and founded the University of Virginia. Those are the things on his tomb at Monticello.

To this humble man Paul the greatest privilege was given "to preach to the Gentiles the unsearchable riches of Christ." Preaching the gospel, teaching the people, winning the lost is not an irksome, disagreeable drudgery. It is a thing of the greatest joy, the most priceless privilege. We are not "quarry slaves scourged to our dungeon at night," and driven to our task in the morning, but ambassadors of the King who go in His name and authority to offer amnesty to all who will honor our royal master.

> "O worship the King all glorious above,
> And gratefully sing of His wonderful love,
> Our shield and defender, the ancient of days,
> Pavillioned in splendor and girded with praise."

In the eighth verse of the third chapter Paul comes to his supreme mission and paramount theme—"To proclaim the unsearchable riches of Christ." I once heard a man waste thirty or forty minutes trying to preach to a great audience on "What's The Big Idea?" But if there was any big idea from him or those he quoted, it was never evident to the audience. How long will it take to exhaust "The Unsearchable Riches of Christ"? How about His essential deity, eternity, incarnation, Virgin Birth, sinless life, vicarious death, triumphant resurrection, boundless compassion, manifold ministries, His place in the home, at the marriage altar, in the shop, in the marts of trade, His words to rulers, His appreciation of women, His love of children, His observation of flowers and animals, His mastery as a teacher, His behavior at weddings and funerals, His skill as a story teller, His manner and charm as a preacher, His reverence for the Scriptures, His dogmatic certitude on all subjects, His astounding claims of sinlessness and limitless power, His capacity for friendship, His patience with stupid disciples, His impatience with self-righteous Pharisees, His joy in bearing the cross, His tenderness with contrite sinners—and ten thousand other things that a ministry of a hundred years could not adequately treat?

The unforgettable sermons one has heard grew out of themes about Jesus. Campbell Morgan at Norfok, Va., on *Ye are that ye may*—"Ye are an elect race, a royal priesthood, a holy nation, a people for God's own possession that ye may show forth the excellences of Him"; etc., Carroll at Hot Springs on *The Pre-eminence of Christ;* Truett at Ashville on *"Christ the Power of God and the Wisdom of God";* Dargan at Monroe, Ga., during a convention, on *The Lamb of God;* J. N. Hall in Jackson, Tenn., on *"If any man sin we have an advocate with the Father";* Billy Sundy in Newport News on *"This poor man cried and the Lord heard him and delivered him out of all his troubles";* Dr. Walker, the Negro preacher of Augusta, Ga., at Hot Springs, Ark., on *God as the Leader of Righteous Causes;* Dr. Phillips of London at the Baptist World Alliance in Philadelphia on *Grace and Glory*. Carroll preached an hour and thirty-five minutes, but all were oblivious of the time. I followed a man in a pastorate who attracted a Jew to his congregation. One day in discussing the preacher, the Jew said to a group of persons: "I shust like dat man, Dr. Blank—he no preach so much of this Jesus Christ doctrine!" One fears that that preacher was under the curse of "preaching another gospel which is not another." Some things need to be rebuked and we must speak reproving words occasionally, and current events may be used helpfully, but the gospel is positive, the cross is a fact, Christ is the center of all riches, the Christian life is spiritual romance, our faith challenges the impossible. We are explorers of a limitless domain of truth that is never commonplace unless our stupidity makes it so. Our sustaining power is greater than atomic energy—"the unsearchable riches of Christ" Paul called it.

Riches is a word to conjure with. The race for riches is the chief curse of our present society. We sing:

"Lord I care not for riches,
    Neither silver nor gold,
I would make sure of heaven,
    I would enter the fold."

Then we grovel in the dirt of dishonesty to lay up treasures where moth and rust corrupt and thieves pillage and steal. We are as covetous as King Midas who inveigled from his god the power to turn to gold everything he touched, then had to hurry back to his tin deity and beg for the removal of the supreme bane of his life.

Socrates, who died 399 years before Christ, was wiser than his generation about material and spiritual things. Hear him: "O Athenians I honor and love you, but I shall obey God rather than you, and as long as I breathe and am able I shall not cease studying philosophy and exhorting you and warning anyone of you I may happen to meet, saying, as I have been accustomed to do, O best of men, seeing you are an Athenian, of a city the most powerful and most renowned for wisdom and strength, are you not ashamed of being careful for riches, how you may acquire them in great abundance and for glory and honor, but care not nor take any thought for wisdom and truth, and for your soul, how it may be made most perfect?" We do not know how much content Socrates intended to put in his words, but Solomon in somewhat similar language personified wisdom as "the principal thing, therefore with all thy getting, get wisdom." There are true riches for which men should strive. "The soul of riches is the riches of the soul." Rome perished through cupidity and corruption. America's present pace in liquor and licentiousness, in lust for lucre, and lure to lawlessness makes a neck and neck race with the Empire of the Caesars.

For "unsearchable" a picturesque word is used. It is a compound of three parts; a preposition which is used here as a negative, a preposition which means "out," and a form which comes from a word that means to "track" or "trace out." It is something that cannot be tracked or traced out. It is inexhaustible, unexplorable, incomputable. The picture is like a man walking in seven league boots exploring continuous diamond mines. He finds diamond mines here, diamond mines there, diamond mines behind him, diamonds before him, diamonds to the right of him, diamonds to the left of him, diamonds rolling under his feet, diamonds blinding his eyes by flashing in the sun light, diamonds everywhere he has been and everywhere he may go. He hurries and races from dawn of day to set of sun, and the next day and on and on he makes millions of tracks but his feet come no nearer to the endless domain of diamonds.

No one can measure Christ; there is no standard of comparison. You cannot evaluate Him for there is no exchange that is priceless with which you may tell His worth. You cannot weigh His moral worth which is greater than that of all material creations and all angelic spirits and all human kind.

The Lord Christ is not only rich, He is riches multiplied, inexhaustible, incalculable. The picture in this word "unsearchable" might be set forth as a maze, and endless domain, a wilderness of beauty and loveliness through which explorers could never find their way, but in which they are lost in wonder and praise.

You had as well try to measure the waters of all the seven seas, count the grains of sand in all the sandy beaches, reckon the number of leaves with their opalescent dew drops, find out how many flowers in all the world's pampas and savannahs are born to blush unseen, or tell the innumerable stars in their courses, as to try to explore and expound all the riches, and beauty and loveliness of Jesus our Lord. David had a hint of it when he desired to "behold the beauty of the Lord and to inquire in His temple." Kepler was worshipping the Lord with his mind when he exclaimed: "O God I think Thy thoughts after Thee." Milton was in the royal spiritual succession when he prayed:

"That to the height of this great argument
I may assert eternal Providence
And justify the ways of God to men."

The apostle tells it again in Rom. 11:33: "O the depth of the riches both of the wisdom and the knowledge of God, how unsearchable (same Greek word as in our

text), are His judgments, and his ways past tracing
out."

Paul was not afraid of universal terms when applied
to Jesus. An unlimited personality justifies unqualified
expression in describing Him. He claimed everything
for his Lord. He prays for all Christians who had not
seen his face "that they may know the mystery of God,
even Christ, in whom are all the treasures of wisdom
and knowledge hidden." A preacher said to an audience
recently: "Jesus went forth to see if He could find out
what plan God had devised to save men." That stuff
does not belong to Paul's conception of one who holds
a monopoly on wisdom and knowledge. Strange to
say that brother was exhorting his hearers to go forth
to build a Christian order in the world. But if that is the
size of Christ, a Christian order would not be effective
if built.

His Mission Was to Turn on the Light

This mighty man of God says that his commission of
grace to preach the unsearchable riches of Christ to the
Gentiles included the privilege of causing the light to
shine out, or to reveal what is the dispensation of the
mystery which has been hidden from the ages in God
who created all things. There is no egotism in that, or
posing as a mighty Atlas upholding a world on his
shoulders. It is the grateful acknowledgment of His
divine commission; the joyful acceptance of the task to
which grace had appointed him. He was fortified by
the deathless conviction that the Lord who had desig-
nated him for the work could bring all things to pass
through His servant. This man could look the world
and the devil in the eyes and say: "I can do all things
through Christ who strengtheneth me." He gloried in

the privilege of heralding abroad the dispensation of the mystery which had been shut up in the heart of God from the eternal ages.

Another meaning of the word translated "dispensation" is "stewardship." The Greek word literally means the work or office of a house steward or servant. That may be the correct meaning here. That would suit Paul's idea of the stewardship of the gospel for himself and for others—"stewards of the manifold grace of God." He was ready to proclaim himself debtor both to the Greeks and to barbarians, and to preach the gospel to the wise and the unwise.

We shall not be in the Pauline succession unless we accept the same grace and obligation to proclaim the mystery of Christ to the whole earth. The stewardship of the grace of God is not alone an exalted privilege but a soul-sobering responsibility as well. No wonder this great heart cried out: "For we are a sweet savor of Christ unto God, in them that are saved, and in them that perish, to the one a savor from death unto death, to the other a savor from life unto life and who is sufficient for these things" (II Cor. 2: 15, 16).

The late Dr. Ellis Fuller was reported to have said: "It may be better for Southern Baptists not to have a Centennial Session of the Southern Baptist Convention, for we might spend a week bragging about what we have done when we have done nothing worth bragging about. After a hundred years of the Convention's life we have fewer than a hundred missionaries on our foreign fields. (Many under appointment were at home because of conditions in foreign countries. We now have 931). If the convention is to take that course it were far better that it never assemble." Southern Baptists have evinced no very great determination to turn on the light of

Christ in the whole world that men may see their way to the cross and to the open grave, and behold the parousia when the Lord shall return in glory, bringing His saints with him.

A Cosmic Purpose

We have to widen our thinking to keep up with Paul's conception of the gospel. His views are cosmic in sweep. In Colossians (1:16-17) he says: "In Him were all things created in the heavens and upon the earth, things visible and things invisible, whether thrones or dominions or principalities or powers, all things have been created through Him, and unto Him, and He is before all things, and in Him all things consist," or hold together. The preaching of the gospel is destined to affect everything and everybody in earthly places and in heavenly realms.

The universal purpose expressed here is: "In order that there might now be made known to the principalities and the powers in the heavenly places through the church, the manifold wisdom of God." Dr. Robertson thinks "the principalities and the powers" refers to the Gnostic heretical teaching. They taught much as "Christian Science" does that matter is evil, and that God could not approach it, so, they said, there were eons, spirits, principalities and powers that came in between God and matter to create it. However it seems better in this passage to refer these things to the good angels and spirits and powers of the heavenly world. Peter says: "Concerning which salvation the prophets sought and searched diligently—which things angels desire to look into" (I Pet. 1:12). They in time will be enlightened through the church. The preaching of the gospel through the church will affect two worlds, and will inform the angels about the manifold wisdom of God in saving men, according to his purpose of the ages which he purposed in Christ Jesus our Lord. Until the people of God face up to the delightful task of universal proclamation of the gospel they will live at a dying rate.

Privilege of Bold Access

This least-of-all-saints-man announces our present privileges in Christ. "In whom we have boldness and access in sure confidence through faith in him" (verse 12). Faith in Christ shows that we are in that eternal purpose, for the purpose was made in Christ Jesus. It introduces us into those "unsearchable riches" in Christ for He is riches inexhaustible. The Greek word for "boldness" means "freedom of speech, telling out every word." Those who keep back something when they talk to God are not free. When we tell the Lord all He gives us all. Believers in Him need not come with bated breath and halting tongue. In Hebrews the fourth chapter the author (Apollos I should guess) used the word translated boldness here. "Let us come boldly (with freedom of speech) to the throne of grace that we may obtain mercy and find grace to help in time of need," (opportune grace for our need). The miracle of all miracles of operating grace is God's ability to justify a sinner through faith in Christ, and cleanse his conscience and give him boldness and assurance. We have this freedom and access now. He uses a present tense. It is the present possession of the believer in the Lord. We have this freedom and boldness in "full confidence," his word implies. His tense of the verb indicates that we have a continuing state of confidence. Well may those tremble who base their salvation on baptism, on their works, on their good character, on the authority of a church, on their genealogy, on their blue blood, red blood or royal blood rather than on the blood of Christ. There is full confidence in the Lord Jesus for every sinner who will tell it all to Him and take by faith Him who is our Redeemer, our life, our resurrection from the dead, our vindicator at the judgment and our eternal salvation.

IX

GRACE FILLS BELIEVERS WITH GOD

Chapter 3:14-19

In this section of chapter three Paul returns from a long detour, but he comes without mud on his wheels or any dents in his fenders. Unlike some of us preachers he says marvelous things on his detours, and different from us he knows how to come back to the highway and go ahead where he left off, as he does here.

He knew logic and rules as few have known them but knew that rules were his servant and not his master. It is well to know Homiletics and also when to disregard it. Dr. E. C. Dargan said in the Homiletics class one day: "He is mighty small man who can't run over a rule when it gets between him and a lost soul."

At the fourteenth verse the apostle returns to the same phrase he used in the first verse: "For this cause." He must have said what he started out to say, for he begins with the same words and goes on to the very climax of prayer. "For this cause I bow my knees unto the Father, from whom every family in heaven and upon the earth is named that He may give unto you according to the riches of His glory to be strengthened with power through His Spirit in the inner (the inside) man, that Christ may dwell through faith in your hearts, ye being rooted and grounded in love, in order that ye may be able to comprehend with all the saints what is the breadth and length and height and depth, and to know the love of Christ which far surpasses knowledge, that ye may be filled unto all the fulness of God."

This is a remarkable prayer any way you may consider it. Paul tells the cause or the object for which he would pray. He says he bows his knees before the Father. That does not have to mean that he was on his knees then, although he may have been. It expresses his habit of prayer, the fact that he was praying then. We do not have to kneel to pray, although at times we may prefer to kneel. But no posture or formality constitutes prayer. To become obsessed of a posture may put too much stress on the physical element. If one felt too proud to kneel to God then surely he should do so. But Paul prayed in the Philippian jail lying on his back; on the highway at Ephesus he kneeled with the elders and friends of the church. Hezekiah prayed lying on his bed, and lived fifteen years. Moses sat on a rock in the attitude of prayer all the day long and defeated the Amalekites. Judson prayed lying down with his feet in the stocks in a Burmese prison. But nobody prays unless his soul cries to God. He prays here to the Father, but he would not have hesitated to pray to Christ, for he repeatedly called Jesus God.

God is "the Father from whom every family in heaven and upon earth is named." "Family" here means "family, tribe, gens, or race." That is, the family idea comes from God's relation to all kindreds, and peoples. Not that He is the spiritual Father of all men, but He is creator of all and cares for all.

When Paul comes to the body of the prayer he sets out four of the greatest things ever asked of God, and they are all arranged in order of a climax. The first plea is that they might be strengthened with power in the "inside man" according to the riches of God's glory. The second was that Christ might dwell through faith in their hearts. This grew out of the first one and is dependent upon it. Third, that they being rooted and grounded in love, may be well able to comprehend with all the saints what is the breadth, length, height and depth and to know the knowledge-surpassing love of Christ. This goes on in climactic fashion from the second and depends on it. Then he reaches the fourth which is the greatest thing he ever could ask: "In order that ye may be filled with all the fulness of God." This results from fulfillment of the first three requests.

There is material here for a half dozen sermons, but let us glance at the four petitions of this greatest of prayers of men. "That ye may be strengthened with power through His Spirit in the inner man according to the riches of His glory." The word here means "strengthened with conquering strength" with power through His Spirit in the inner man. There is no conquering strength save through the power of the Holy Spirit. All power that is not His power is weakness. All plans not His plans will fail. All wisdom not His wisdom is ignorance that will blight and delude. He knoweth the deep things of God which we can never know except as He reveals them.

Our Lord Himself was dependent on the Spirit and wrought His works through Him. Luke barely got started in Acts till in the second verse of the first chapter he says: "Until the day He was taken up after He gave commandment through the Holy Spirit to the apostles whom He chose." In the fifth verse the Spirit-directed Lord tells the apostles they shall be baptized in the Holy Spirit; and in the eighth verse He informs

them that they shall "receive power when the Holy
Spirit has come upon them." Not "after" the Spirit
has come upon you as the King James Version reads,
but the "Holy Spirit coming upon you." He *is* the
power. The brethren of the Jerusalem church in making
their missionary plans said: "It seemed good to the
Holy Spirit and to us." When Paul, Barnabas and
John Mark set forth from Antioch on the first tour,
Luke says that they were sent forth by the Holy Spirit.

He is the Spirit of wisdom and revelation. We know
not what to say or how to say it without His guidance.
He is the Spirit of might and we have no strength
except as He gives it. He is the Spirit of life and there
is no life except as He quickens from the dead. He
is the Presence who went with Moses through the
wilderness, the Revelator who taught Isaiah of the
suffering Servant; the Sanctifier who claimed and de-
voted John the Baptist from the womb.

The apostle asks that the strength and the power of
the Spirit be given to them according to the riches of
the Father's glory. That is according to the riches of
His character. It is according to the plentitude of His
power. It is according to His matchless mercy. It is
according to the greatness of His goodness. "The riches
of His glory" is the wealth of His personality, His
being, which is composed of all His wisdom, power,
grace, goodness, and love. The very character and
benevolence of the Father are requisitioned through
the Spirit whom He asks for them.

Men act upon one another from without. The Spirit
of God acts upon us within. He can find entrance to
all the dark places and all the hidden sanctuaries of
the soul. He carries the key that will unlock all the
heart's mysteries. His quiet voice stills all our fears.

His healing balm solaces all our sorrows. "So dark at times is every life; so full at times of discouragements, of dreariness, of sadness, of loneliness, of bitter memories, and of fading hopes does the human heart become that if we are to be strong we must have a strength that will manifest itself most chiefly in this, that it teaches us how to bear, how to weep, how to submit"—Maclaren.

Christ's Home

In the second request Paul climbs a rung higher in his ascent on the ladder of supplication. "That Christ may dwell in your hearts through faith; ye being rooted and grounded in love." If we are strengthened with power through His Spirit in the inward man according to the first petition then Christ will dwell through faith in our hearts, and we shall be rooted and grounded in love. He is talking about a permanent manner of life, the fixed and continuous residence of Christ in the heart. It is not a pop call or passing salute of the Lord as He might breeze by the believer or the believer might dash along the highway and wave at the Master. But the dear Lord is to live with us. The Greek word means "to make a home," He asks that the Lord may come down to dwell with us, to live in the same house with us, and the house is the human spirit, the heart of our poor being. That means Christ living at the center of our being, at the center of our will, at the center of our desires and purposes, at the center of our affections,ideals and emotions; and our living in His Will in all things. His hand will be on the throttle and control and motivate our power. His wisdom will produce silence or inspire the utterance of our tongue. On the day of Pentecost the disciples "began and continued in orderly discourse as the Holy Spirit kept on giving them utterance." That is about what Luke's Greek means. No wonder they confounded their critics who said: "To what will this thing come?" No wonder Peter unhorsed and confused his accusers of the Sanhedrin by saying: "If we this day be examined because of a good deed done to an impotent man by what power he is made whole be it known unto you all that by the name of Jesus Christ of Nazareth by faith in His name doth this man stand before you whole?"

To put men in jail for helping a sick man is an absurdity that even the devil cannot justify. No wonder they knew not how to answer Peter when they commanded silence about "this name"; and he shot back: "Whether it is right in the sight of God to hearken unto you rather than unto God judge ye, for we cannot but speak the things we have seen and heard." They had to equivocate with: "What shall we do to these men for that a notable miracle has been wrought by them is evident to everybody in Jerusalem and we cannot deny it." Such answers as Peter gave that sound the very depths of truth in life's great crises, are not evoked from men's wisdom, but are given by the indwelling Spirit of God, who by His presence is living, reigning, and residing in the heart. Let it be repeated that Paul was praying that Christ might make His home in their hearts. Jesus was orphaned and neglected when here in the flesh and had no certain dwelling place, no home. He wants a home now in the spirit of men. What fellowship, what love, what confidence and sense of security there is in having a home. A father took his little boy on his lap and badgered and bantered him, saying: "Boy, you are no-account, you don't work enough to pay your board." With a smile on his ruddy face and a twinkle in his big brown eyes he said, in his bad English: "Well, but though, I guess I ain't no boarder, I *live here*." What a difference in sojourning, and living in a place, in being under limitations and dwelling in our own house, where we have rights and privileges. Our Lord wants a home and we need Him as our permanent guest, and guide.

This continuous dwelling of the Lord in our hearts will come through faith. He lives with all who believe in Him. His fellowship is not broken if our faith is constant. We ourselves love to be with those who believe in us. We are glad to please them and serve them. True faith, constant perennial faith, means an abiding, omnipotent Christ in the heart with all his ministries of love and power.

Another part of this prayer of the apostle, which results from fulfilment of the first part, is put under the two figures of a well rooted tree and a solidly based foundation—"ye being thoroughly, perfectly rooted (he uses a perfect passive participle to express the idea of completeness) and founded (same tense) in love." We think, at once of "He shall be like a tree planted by the streams of water that bears its fruit in season and its leaf shall not wither."

Olive trees planted in the days of Constantine still weather the winds and stem the storms of Palestine. The cedars of Lebanon and the redwoods and sequoias of California have stood since the memory of man runneth not to the contrary. But these are not so majestic and mighty as the soul, that on Jesus has leaned for repose, the soul that He cannot and will not desert to its foes.

The other figure is "perfectly founded" in love. New York skyscrapers are founded on fifty or sixty feet of pilings driven in the earth with concrete poured in to make a solid base of stone all around and over the strong boles of the timbers, so that the steel structure which rises a thousand feet in the air and sways and careens several feet from the heat and the wind cannot be uprooted or toppled from its foundation.

The memorable and warning words of Jesus come to mind: "Every one therefore who hears these my own words and does them shall be likened unto a wise man who built his house on the rock; and the rain came down and the rivers came and the winds blew and fell against that house and it did not fall, for it was founded (perfect tense as in our text) upon the rock. And every one who hears these my words and is not doing them shall be likened unto a foolish man who built his house upon the sand. And the rain came down and the rivers came and the winds blew and beat upon that house and it fell and the ruin of it was great" (Matt. 7:24-27). Multitudes fall today being unable to endure the heat, the drouth and the burdens of life because they are not planted by the streams of water and are not founded upon the rock.

"Love endureth all things," and "endure" means to "wear out." Moses endured as seeing Him who is invisible. His heroic, stupendous work, his enduring the impatience and contradiction of complaining Israel, would have been impossible without his being strengthened with power in the "inside man," and without his unfailing vision of Him who is invisible.

Love suffereth long and is kind. It knows how to stand under the load and modulate its voice and show a kindly smile that comes from the heart. Love hopeth all things. It is an incurable optimist that knows that if things are not right, they shall be righted in the good providence of the God of hope. Love believeth all things, therefore can learn, for increase in true knowledge and wisdom is impossible apart from faith. Love knows that tongues without toil are an empty sound, that prophecy without profound sympathy is piffle, that faith without loving fellowship is false, that charity without mercy is a misnomer, that martyrdom without benevolent ministry is meaningless and unrewarded. Love is long suffering, or has a big spirit, is long-tempered. Love shows kindness. Love is not envious, does not get boiling hot with jealousy. Love is no braggart, no "swashbuckler" who brandishes the sword. Love is not guilty of bad taste or moral indecency. Love does not even seek the things of itself, is not intent on its own advantage, does not consider or contemplate doing evil. She does not rejoice in wrong, but does rejoice in and with the truth. Love endures all, believes all, hopes all, suffers all. Love never at any time falls out or is hissed off the stage. Prophecies shall be abolished, tongues will cease, knowledge shall be done away with, but love never; for we have come to know in part and in part we prophesy, but when complete, full grown maturity has come, then the partial shall be abolished. When I was a child, as a child I talked, as a child I thought, as a child I reasoned, but now that I have become a man I abolished the things of the child. For up to this minute we are looking through a mirror in a riddle, or enigma, but then (we shall see) face to face. Now I know in part, but then I shall know well even as I was well known. And now there abide faith, hope, love, these three but the greatest of these is love. Love does all these things and more according to the need of the hour, and those who are perfectly rooted and grounded in love, having the conquering strength of the Spirit's power and the consequent abiding Lord

making His home in the life will exemplify the miracle-
working efficiency of love which never faileth.

> "Had I the tongues of Greek and Jews
> And nobler speech than angels use;
> If love be absent, I am found
> Like tinkling brass, an empty sound.
>
> Were I inspired to preach and tell
> All that is done in heaven and hell,
> Or could my faith the world remove
> Still I am nothing without love.
>
> Should I distribute all my store
> To feed the hungry, clothe the poor,
> Or give my body to the flame
> To gain a martyr's glorious name;
>
> If love to God and love to men
> Be absent, all my hopes are vain;
> Nor tongues nor gifts, nor fiery zeal
> The work of love can e'er fulfil"
>
> —Author Unknown

The Third Petition

The apostle asks that the first two petitions of his
prayer be fulfilled "in order that ye may be well able
to comprehend with all the saints what is the breadth
and length and height and depth, and to know the
knowledge-surpassing love of Christ." The word translated "comprehend" is used in classic Greek to mean
"lay hold of, or seize with the purpose of conquering,
or possessing or making one's own." From that idea
there comes the meaning, no doubt, of conquering or
possessing with the mind, or to understand or comprehend.

Height and depth are the same thing reaching in two directions, so here we have the three dimensions of the love of Christ. It reaches up to the resplendent and eternal throne. It is the very essence and being of God himself, for God is love. It goes down to the immeasureable depravity, and fathomless depths of man's sin. Never did height and depth connect two more disparate, and divided things than here. Never were two so infinitely removed positive and negative poles of personality united in such unity and harmony as here. It is the incomparable love of God, the incomprehensible love of God, the unexplorable love of God, the imponderable love of God, the unmerited love of God, the amazing love of God, to which there is nothing else like or equal in heaven above or on the earth beneath. It is that which the saints know by experience better than they know anything else, yet they do not understand. It may be that "comprehend" is a little too strong a word to use in describing our knowledge here. "Also to apprehend with all the saints," or "able to possess with all the saints" might be better and more within our reach. We can apprehend that which we cannot fully comprehend. We can possess that which we do not quite understand. We can delight in the lark's morning song that greets the day with gladness but cannot comprehend it all. We can know and love the nightingale's vesper hymn which closes the gates of day, but cannot fathom all its music. We cannot "burnish the rose, paint the lily and gild the sunbeam" with the brush of human genius, but we can quaff the perfume of the rose, behold nature's tinting of the lily and find the seven rainbow hues in the sunbeam. We cannot comprehend the guileless innocence of a sleeping baby that smiles as it hears the song of angels, but we are subdued and blessed in beholding the child. You cannot sound, or weigh, or measure, or diagram, or comprehend your mother's love, but your heart rests in the sure confidence of her affection.

There are two kinds of knowledge. The Bible uses two words in two shades of meaning: To know or to perceive with the mind, and to know by experience or feel in the heart, conscience and affections. Paul in one place says knowledge puffs up. That is knowledge gained through the intellect but misused. Intellectual knowledge is good if used spiritually. The knowledge that puffs up is the conceit of human learning. In another place he says: "Love builds up." Love that builds up is knowledge taught by the Spirit of God. Perception of the mind is good if used lawfully, but it cannot fathom and compass the spiritual. The natural man knoweth not the things of the spirit. They must be spiritually discerned. The most glorious sunrise and picturesque landscape have no significance for a blind man. A deaf man has no concern for music. The knowledge of experience is the highest, purest, best knowledge.

The knowledge of experience can appreciate and understand personality, but personality defies all intellectual effort and processes of analysis. Knowledge of experience can understand because it is motivated by love. We have information and give credence or testimony about any person or subject, but that is not enough. We must go on to the point of confidence and trust if we enter into the real secret of experiential knowledge. There must be not only assent of the intellect but consent of the heart, and that is faith, and that leads to serene confidence or love which casteth out fear.

"Comprehend with all the saints" sounds a heart throb of a great family. There is a wealth in the communal love of the Savior. When a worshipper can hear the glad acclaim of ten thousand other Spirits who present their devotion to God the volume is great and the melody is sweeter. When one thinks of a great family, a multitude, a countless host, who lived in the past, who now survive, who shall follow us hereafter, who bow before His throne and pay loving devotion to the Lord of all, the prospect enhances the glory of the scene. Then one heart's adoration and praise will help that of another. As iron sharpeneth iron so doth the face of man that of his fellow. Heat applied to the molecules in one end of a piece of iron will soon be transmitted to the whole bar of steel. A drop of water falling in the ocean becomes a part of the whole and the whole becomes a part of it. "The strength of the pack is the wolf and the strength of the wolf is the pack." One can chase a thousand and two can put ten thousand to flight. The ratio is tremendous which will soon raise the quantity to the nth power, which defies calculation.

To be a humble member of the body of Christ is glory ineffable. Neither does it matter what member it is, for every member is priceless for its purpose. "I want to be an eye for beauty and light," demands an ambitious foot; but he forgets that men cannot walk with their eyes. "I want to be an ear, to hear sweet melodies of harps," pipes a finger, oblivious of the fact that without fingers harps cannot sound. "I want to be a tongue to speak eloquent words" says a hand, but suppose there were no hand to turn words into deeds. Another would be racing feet to carry the runner to victory, but athletes without eyes to see the course and

ears to hear the signals were no better than lame dogs
in the chase. It does not matter what member we are
if we only help carry Christ to victory. Don't worry
and fret because you cannot be all or have what you
think the most important place. Remember that "in
heaven all God's chillun is goin' to have shoes."

A supreme lesson here—and pray do not forget it—
is that only saints, that is true believers, can know the
love of Christ which passes knowledge. Sanctity of
character is a condition of this knowledge. Light
doesn't come through smoky windows. The sun seen
through colored glasses will be the color of the glass.
Fog on the wind shield will snare the chauffeur to col-
lision and crash of death. The vision of the stars fades
away if the lens of the telescope is soiled or the mirror
clouded by human breath. "Blessed are the pure in
heart, for they shall see God." If thine eye be single
the whole body shall be full of light. Our supreme danger
here is that we shall fix these rules on others and not
take our own measure. The clarity of *my* vision depends on having singleness of eye. The strength of *my*
life is gauged by obedience to Christ.

Maclaren says: "We have no means by which we can
estimate the darkness, and the depth of the misery from
which we have been delivered, nor the height and
the radiance of the glory to which we are to be lifted.
And until we can tell and measure by our compasses
both of these two extremes of possible human fate, till
we have gone down into the deepest abyss of a bottom-
less pit of growing alienation and misery, and up above
the highest of all unending progress into light and glory
and God-likeness, we have not stretched our compasses
wide enough to touch the two poles of this great sphere,
the infinite love of Jesus Christ. So we bow before it,

we know that we possess it with a knowledge more sure and certain, more deep and valid than our knowledge of aught but ourselves; but yet it is beyond our grasp, and towers above us inaccessible in the altitude of its glory, and stretches deep beneath us in profundity of its condescension."

"But none of the ransomed ever knew
How deep were the waters crossed,
Or how dark the night the Lord passed through
Ere he found his sheep that was lost."

The Divine Fulness

Now gather up the apostle's expansive thought for his supreme climax. His heart-longing for them was that they might be made strong by his Spirit in the inner man, that Christ might dwell in their hearts through faith, that they might be well able to comprehend with all the saints the breadth, length, the height and depth and to know the knowledge-surpassing love of Christ, "*in order* that ye may be filled with all the fulness of God." That is the superlative of infinity. It is a measure which is beyond all measurement. That contemplates putting an ocean in a little lake. It is like putting the blinding light and withering heat of the sun in the flickering flame of a candle. When we read of Christ: "In Him dwelt all the fulness of the God-head bodily" we are not surprised. That is just what we expected for he is very God of very God. But infinity dwelling in the finite is baffling to our comprehension. Yet that is what Paul plainly says. How can this be? Well, a child may have all the fulness of his father's being and personality. He may be filled with his father's mind, illustrate his father's disposition, be a repetition of his father's personality, prejudices and predilections in such

facsimile likeness that we say the father lives in his son
and the son lives in his father. This illustration can
suggest but cannot explain the mystery, for as much
alike as the father and son may be, there is no power
that completely unites the two as God and the believer
are united through the Spirit's ministry of the divine
fulness in the saint's willing spirit. In interpreting this
scripture we must get away from measurements of
material things. It is impossible for a world or a planet
to be compressed into a cockle shell. Here we are
dealing with spiritual quantities which defy weights and
measurements and dimensions. A child can have all its
father's love. The fulness of one personality can dwell
in another personality. Unlimited power can take possession of weakness. Full-orbed and comprehensive wisdom
can communicate itself to ignorance or limited knowledge.

A thoroughly practical thing that Paul is asking
here is that God's saints shall be absolutely and completely filled with God. As William Booth said: "God
had all there was of William Booth." As some one said
to a seeker after Christ who indicated he would give
the whole world to have the Master: "That is exactly
what He will cost you." The great life of Dr. J. B.
Tidwell was based in the motto of his young manhood:
"J. B. Tidwell plus God is sufficient for any task." The
same omnipotence was the boast of Paul which he set
in the record: "I can do all things through Christ who
strengthens me."

Since Paul is dealing here with infinite spiritual quantity he may be taking into his thought the sweep of
eternity also, and setting forth an experience which
begins with the saints, and makes great progress in time
and projects itself into coming ages for its complete

fulfillment. All the fulness of the God-head bodily dwells in Christ now and Christ dwells in His people now, and the body of Christ is growing now in ever expanding numbers and in the growing sanctification of the redeemed, God's family. Paul's concept here is the fulness of God in all the saints. Now if the body of Christ is increased by every being who accepts Him, His body will continue to grow until all the redeemed are completely saved, sanctified and glorified without spot or wrinkle or any such thing. When that which is perfect is come, His body shall be complete and comprehensive enough to contain all the fulness of Christ who contains all the fulness of God; and this greatest of human supplications will be fulfilled and the unity of the Father and Christ and His people for which our Lord prayed in the garden will be completely realized in glory.

> "Come Thou Almighty King,
> Help us Thy name to sing,
> Help us to praise:
> Father all glorious,
> O'er all victorious,
> Come and reign over us,
> Ancient of days.
>
> Come Holy Comforter,
> Thy sacred witness bear
> In this glad hour;
> Thou who almighty art,
> Now rule in every heart,
> And ne'er from us depart,
> Spirit of power."

X

THE GREAT DOXOLOGY OF GRACE

Eph. 3:20, 21

The last two verses of chapter three of Ephesians might be, not inappropriately, called the apex of praise. While the magnifying of God's grace has run all through the three chapters this brief section is more especially the ascription to God Himself of the highest praise of His power and of the loftiest expression of His eternal glory, which will be manifested through the ages in the church and in Christ Jesus, its glorious redeemer, founder and head. This halleluiah chorus of praise is characteristic of Paul's spirit throughout Ephesians and in other epistles. But he pauses at the end of this chapter to look back over the previous paragraph with its revelation of the mystery of Christ for all nations, the great love wherewith God loved us, the raising up of the dead with Christ, the publishing of God's manifold wisdom by the church, and the bold access of all saints to God through Christ, that he might exhaust his brain and empty his heart in a definite, though inadequate, effort to give due glory to God for His power, mercy, and love.

As to the text itself he begins the twentieth verse with the definite article (the) which can refer to none but God about whom he has spoken so wonderfully in the foregoing paragraph. The context also shows that the reference is to God for no other one can do what is ascribed to Him. The apostle says: "To the One who is able to do above all things, superabundantly beyond what we ask or think according to the power which is now working in us." The text does not mean "The One who can do superabundantly above all things which we ask or think." He first ascribes all power, unlimited efficiency, absolute omnipotence to God—"To the One who can do above all things." His power goes beyond all things, covers and controls all creation, includes all range of possibilities, and far more. His power is total, absolute, unlimited, undefeatable, inherent and underived from any source. This power He exercises in our behalf. The meaning is: "Who is able to do beyond all things: to do superabundantly beyond what we ask or think."

The Expositor's Greek Testament correctly says: "We have two distinct descriptions of God here, the second of which explains and develops the thought of the first. He is described, first generally, in respect of the absoluteness of His power, as able to do beyond all things, able to do more than all, that is, one of whose efficiency there is no limit; and then with more particular reference to the case of Paul and his fellow believers (and we would add case of us also) as able to do above all measure beyond anything with which our asking or even our thinking is conversant; superabundantly beyond the utmost requests we can make in prayer, nay beyond all that can suggest itself to our minds in their highest ventures." There is an unlimited wealth of God's power which we have never tapped; a field, a continent of His love and mercy we have not explored, even our eyes have not seen, or our minds dreamed of.

A Negro deacon whimsically remarked about his new Pastor: "He has done asked the Lord for a heap of things what that last preacher didn't know the Lord had." So he truly may have done, and the next preacher who comes may do likewise, and the next and the next, but no one or all combined will touch the bottom of God's barrel of bounty, or break through the surface layer of God's universal store of immeasurable mercies. Our praying is so superficial and trivial that it should shame us. Of course we will not ask God for foolish things, or selfish things, or things inconsistent with His honor or His being. But let us not fear to put our thought, our life, our best in the effort. One heard a boiler-maker from Chicago pray in a Mississippi revival so much like an apostle ought to pray that the spell it put on the spirit has remained through four decades. A prayer in the Southern Baptist Convention at Baltimore, in 1940, by B. D. Gray, when he was approaching ninety years of age, was the most talked about occurrence of that meeting. The prayer of F. C. McConnell after Truett's sermon at Asheville, N. C., in the 1902 convention put us all lower on our faces before God than even the mighty sermon had done. The marvelous spiritual fervor and dynamic power of a praying woman in, perhaps, the most revolutionary revival one ever conducted must have had more to do with the results than all the three weeks' preaching. It was impossible for that meeting to have failed with such praying in it. But none of these, or Paul, or John, or Mary the Lord's Mother, or Polycarp, Irenaeus, Augustine, Chrysostom (John of Antioch), Athanasius, Luther, Huss or Hubmeyer, Bunyan, Carey, Judson, Spurgeon, Broadus, or Carroll ever began to sound the limitless depths of God's power to do exceedingly abundantly beyond all they ever asked or dreamed that God has in His infinite love for His children.

"According to the power which is (now) working in us" must refer to the conscious presence of the Holy

Spirit in our hearts. Do pray, in the name of the Lord, put away the notion that the Holy Spirit is a vague "influence" on the outside of us rather than God Himself in the person of the Spirit who dwells in believers. The indwelling Spirit is the greatest fact, and ought to be the most precious reality in the heart of all believers. Paul is saying that because of the indwelling Spirit, who is our Teacher, Interpreter, and Guide, we know by His revelation in our soul that God is able to do for us vastly more than our feeble intellect can imagine or our halting tongues can tell.

Now to such a Being as that is it not fitting, is it not just, is it not honorable, is it not joyful, and supremely ecstatic that we give praise, adoration, worship and glory? Paul thinks it is so, and he shouts with great emphasis: "Unto HIM be the glory in the church and in Christ Jesus."

"In the church and in Christ Jesus" must be the correct text. The King James Version says: "In the church by Christ Jesus," but we should supply the word "and," making "and in Christ Jesus." This is according to the best manuscripts and the best Greek texts. Westcott and Hort, and Nestle's text which are before me both have "and." The American Standard translation has "and in Christ Jesus." This is sufficiently conclusive. Then it is agreeable to Paul's general teaching. God's glory is in His church, and in His Son.

The word "ecclesia," "church," used here, like words in all languages, is used in different senses, or shades of meaning. It was in constant use in the Greek language centuries before Christ was born. It means an "assembly" of persons who were called out from their homes and business to act as a council, or governing body of a city or state, such as that which ruled Athens. It was a free, democratic body, that is, made up of freeholders, who were called out for that purpose. In the New Testament it is used, one thinks, in the abstract, the generic, the particular, and the prospective, or proleptical senses, but these uses do not change the basal, or radical sense of the word. The word occurs in the New Testament 117 times, and all but five (Acts 7:38; 19:32, 39, 41; Heb. 2:12) refer to Christ's ecclesia, or church. "And since Hebrews 2:12, though a quotation from the Old Testament, is prophetic, finding fulfillment in New Testament times, we need not regard it as an exception" (B. H. Carroll). These 113 uses of the word, including Heb. 2:12, refer, one believes, either to the particular assembly of Christ on the earth, or to His general assembly, or church in glory. Nearly all the 113 uses of the word refer to a particular assembly, or church, such as the church at Corinth, or the church at Ephesus. The abstract and generic uses belong to this class. Matthew, 16:18 is the abstract use, referring to the church as an institution, as we say "the school" meaning all schools in a general sense but including each particular school in application of the term.

Another abstract or institutional use of the word is in Ephesians 3:10, 21, where Paul prays that the manifold wisdom of God may be made known to the powers and authorities in the heavenly places through the church. Verse 2:21 ascribes all glory to God who is able to do above all that we ask or think according to the power that is working in us (present tense), "unto Him be the glory in the church and in Christ Jesus forever and ever." God is doing a work through the church now which will bring Him eternal glory. That is the church on earth which Christ commissioned to evangelize the nations.

Matthew 18:17 is the generic use of the word, which tells what kind of tribunal is competent to decide matters between alienated brethren. He does not say what church, but in application it becomes particular and means that every New Testament church is the sole arbiter of differences among its members, and of all matters pertaining to its own life and work.

In Hebrews 12:23; and Ephesians 5:25-27 the reference seems to be to the general assembly of Christ in heaven. But in such cases the assembly is prospective. The general assembly is not yet, but will be only when all the redeemed of all time are raised, and glorified, and assembled in heaven. The church on earth and the triumphant church in glory do not exist simultaneously. The glorified church will not exist until all the saved are regenerated, raised from the dead, completely sanctified in their new bodies, and glorified in heaven as the general assembly and church of the first born whose names are written in the book of life.

A careful study will show that the characteristics of the prospective church in glory are often applied in the New Testament to the church on earth. This is not strange when we remember that every New Testament church on earth, made up of redeemed people, is a part of the general assembly, or church that will appear in glory.

Dr. Broadus said: "In the New Testament the *spiritual* Israel, never actually assembled, is sometimes conceived of as an ideal congregation or assembly, and this is denoted by the word ecclesia," (Commentary on Matthew). He was contrasting "spiritual Israel" with national or carnal Israel." However the same thing is true of the church on earth and the general assembly church in glory.

The work of the church on earth is to call out or win those who shall constitute the heavenly assembly. The only type of the church in glory is the particular assembly, or church, on earth. The New Testament applies such figures as the house of God, "the temple of God," "the body" or "flock" or "bride" of Christ to the church on earth just as freely as it does to the general assembly in heaven. But it never applies these terms to particular assemblies in a *collective* sense. "Ecclesia never applies to all denominations *collectively*, or to all living professors of religion, or to all believers *collectively*." But all the saved will constitute the church in heaven.

In Ephesians, 2:21, 22 Paul says: "In whom each several building, fitly framed together, groweth into a holy temple in the Lord; in whom ye also are builded together for a habitation of God in the Spirit." Every New Testament Church is a temple of God. "So then ye (the Gentiles) are no longer strangers and so-journers, but ye are fellow-citizens with the saints, and of the household of God (literally "and the household of God") being built upon the foundation of the apostles and prophets, Christ Jesus himself being the chief cornerstone; in whom each several building is growing into a holy temple in the Lord. That applies to every congregation or church, separately. Each church is a temple of the Lord; and that is true of the church at Ephesus, or to each church in the Ephesian area, if Ephesians is a circular letter sent to all of them.

In Acts 20:18 Paul said to the elders of the church at Ephesus: "Take heed unto yourselves, and to all the flock (all the members of the Ephesian church), in which the Holy Spirit hath made you bishops, to feed the church of the Lord which He purchased with His own blood." Paul was speaking of the church at Ephesus, not of the church in glory, and not of all churches on earth *collectively* considered, although the principle is true of each one in the application of the truth. Paul must have had reference to a particular church when he discussed the qualifications of bishops and deacons, and the behaviour of women and children, saying: "If a man knoweth not how to rule his own house, how shall he take care of the church of God?"; and again: "That thou mayest know how men ought to behave themselves in the house of God which is the Church of the living God, the pillar and ground of the truth" (1 Tim. Chap. 3).

Again the apostle wrote specifically to "the church of God which is at Corinth" (1 Cor. 3:9) "Ye are God's building," "ye are the temple of God" (1 Cor. 3:16). To this same Corinthian church he wrote (1 Cor. 12:27) "Now ye are the body of Christ and severally members thereof." He goes on to say: "And God hath set some in the church, first apostles, secondly prophets, thirdly teachers," etc., practically the same classification of workers he gives in Ephesians 4:8-12, which latter passage some strangely interpret as referring to a universal invisible church without showing us how it could be possible for apostles, prophets, evangelists, and pastors and teachers to function in a universal, invisible church. Paul was talking about the church at Corinth when he called it "the temple of God, the building of God, and the body of Christ." When he says: "Whether one member suffereth, all the members suffer with it, or one member is honored, all the members rejoice with it" (1 Cor. 12:26) can anybody think that he is speaking of an invisible church on earth, or of the general assembly in glory where all suffering shall have forever passed away?

The more one has studied the question of the particular church and a general church the more has he been convinced that they do not and cannot exist simultaneously. Dr. B. H. Carroll (in *Baptists and Their Doctrines*) has expressed the truth with convincing clarity; and I have profited by his excellent discussion in setting forth my views, which through much thought have become a conviction that this is the teaching of the New Testament.

The commission was given to the church at Jerusalem, which was a going institution before Christ left the earth. This is made plain by Matt. 18:17 where the Lord gave specific command and instructions concerning settlement of personal difficulties among brethren of the church. The church was made the arbiter and sole authority in such matters. The Savior's words would not have been intelligible had the church not been in existence already. God will have infinite and loftiest praise and glory in His church and in Christ Jesus.

With almost extravaganza of words in trying to express his meaning Paul sets forth the eternal quality of God's glory. He says, with special emphasis on the pronoun: "And to *Him* be the glory in the church and in Christ Jesus unto all the generations of the age of the ages"—the strongest way the Greek language can express the idea of eternity.

God's Holy Spirit is now working in us to reveal God's will and more of His power and His works which He will accomplish in His obedient people. Unto *Him* who has such power, unto Him who exercises such mercy, "unto *Him* be *the* glory in the church and in Christ Jesus."

During the World Exposition held in Chicago in 1892 there was *A Congress of Religions,* where the representatives of leading religions of the world met and discussed and commended, each his own faith.

George C. Lorimer of Tremont Temple Baptist Church, of Boston, spoke for the Baptists. He tells the story in his own great way of the last session of that congress. He wrote: "It was on the occasion of the closing service. I had been assigned a place on the platform, and naturally began to inspect my neighbors. There was not far from me, Shibata, High Priest of Shintoism, clothed in priestly robes of white and gold. Then near to him Suami Vivekananda in orange dress, and imposing turban, and in company, some in costume, some in citizen's attire, were Rev. Dr. Momerie of the Church of England, Prince Serge Walkonski of Russia, Bishop Arnett of Africa, Dr. Barrows, Mr. Bonney, and many others, not forgetting my own beloved Dr. George Dana Boardman. Well, when I contemplated the group and thought of the differences it represented, every feeling of elation departed and a strange dejection came over me. Nor can I say that it was diminished, but rather increased, by what I heard. I had not arrived early enough to be exalted by the opening anthem, "Lift Up Your Heads O Ye Gates!", and when the farewell speeches were delivered I was in no mood to appreciate them. As I recall the scene I cannot remember any word derogatory to our Saviour, or, on the part of His disciples, any implied disloyalty in thought or word to Him and to His church. But, I acknowledge, it seems to me more might have been said—something clear, though not controversial, on the subject of His divinity, His atonement—something that would have shown distinctly and impressively, that while we were not indifferent to goodness and wisdom in the sages of Asia, we must adore Him and Him only as the one supreme incarnation of the living God, with whom it were folly to bring into comparison the Zoroasters and Buddhas of the East. Perhaps I expected too much. But the absence of jubilant tone and of lofty enthusiasm for Christ in the addresses of His followers, and of that kind of conquering spirit which sometimes sounds in voice and gleams in manner when even no triumphant words are uttered, oppressed me and rendered me fairly despondent. As my solemn melancholy increased the horrible suspicion seized me that Pilate and Herod were making friends once more, and through their courtesies the Lord would again be crucified. I was startled, alarmed, prostrated by the thought; but just as my despair was gathering into stormful clouds of indignation and my reason lay quite helpless at the feet of my discouraged and darkened imagination, relief was at hand. The Apollo Club, under the direction of Professor Tomlins, sang, and sang magnificiently, 'The Halleluiah Chorus'—

Halleluiah! halleluiah! halleluiah!
He shall reign forever, halleluiah!

"I shall never forget it. All round the galleries the immense choir was distributed, the leader occupying the platform and swaying the voices at his command with superb skill and energy. His soul glistened in his eyes, the sentiment expressed seemed to thrill his entire being, and his own spirit was imparted to singers and audience alike. The voices rose and fell, now soft and sweet as the warbling of a forest of birds, and then loud and firm as the triumphant beat of the waves on the shore. And still the refrain returned.

"He shall reign forever, 'halleluiah,' whispered melo-diously as a hope, thundered assuringly as a prophecy. This chorus marked the highest point of enthusiasm, and it seems to have stirred memories of Christian an-cestry, of Christian sacrifice, and of Christian antici-pation—yea, and of Christ Himself—for the audience broke into tumultuous applause, handkerchiefs waved, and men and women looked as though they believed that the whole earth should yet echo the glad halleluiah song, and Jesus forever reign Lord of lords, and King of kings.

"My despondency had gone, my common sense had returned. I realized the foolish weakness of my fears, and I found myself during the rest of the memorable evening in the depths of my soul crying, 'Halleluiah.'

"Why do the heathen rage and the people imagine a vain thing. 'Halleluiah!'

"Yet have I set my king upon my holy hill of Zion, 'Halleluiah.'

"Ask of me and I shall give thee the heathen for thine inheritance and the unttermost parts of the earth for thy possession 'Halleluiah! halleluiah! halleluiah!'

"God also hath highly exalted Him and given Him a name which is above every name: that at the name of Jesus every knee should bow, of things in heaven and things in the earth and things under the earth. 'Halle-luiah, He shall reign forever.'

"The meeting was over and the crowds disbursing as I went out into the night. I walked alone and hurriedly to my abiding place. As I pushed along, excited, lost in reverie, not one of the speeches I had heard during the evening revived in my memory, but the voices of the chorus followed me:

" 'Halleluiah, He shall reign forever!' When I prayed that night the strain still haunted me, and during my

long journey home, and since then on the streets and in
my study, I have distinctly heard the notes of that
exultant anthem. Nor can I believe I was the only one
in that vast multitude who was thus impressed. Many,
I am persuaded, shared my triumphant mood, and went
forth from the Hall of Columbus, assured, as never in
the past, that Christ must conquer all His foes, and
determined to do more than ever to usher in the glorious
day when 'He shall reign forever, halleluiah.' "

"Unto the One who is able to do above all things,
who is able to do exceeding abundantly above all we
ask or think according to the power which is now working in us, unto HIM be the glory in the church and in
Christ Jesus, Amen."

XI

EFFECTUAL CALLING OF GRACE

Ephesians 4:1-5

Does it seem strange that God, who can do all things, would let His child be a prisoner? I would do almost anything, except deny the Lord, before I would let my child go to prison. God will let His children go to prison when they are doing all in their power to serve and honor Him. He let His good apostles be killed. He let Christians be thrown to the lions while the Roman crowds screamed with delight. He let Polycarp, and John Huss and hundreds more be burned at the stake and never wrought a miracle to save them.

Paul could have said that he was a "prisoner of the Lord" because God's love held him captive. But "the prisoner *in* the Lord" means more. Let us see: He was in the Lord and was a prisoner. Not bad was it? He was in the Lord's power and was a prisoner, and that was not bad. He was in the Lord's service and for that reason was thrown into prison which is perhaps the meaning he intended here. But all these were true. He was in the Lord, in the Lord's power, and in the Lord's service and wicked men put him in prison because he preached the gospel. And the wonderful thing is he did not mind being put in prison for his Lord. He was even glad to suffer for Christ, and turned his prison life to good account to serve the Lord.

When he said: "*The* prisoner in the Lord" he was not

boasting that he was the only prisoner Christ had or the best one, but simply telling what class of men he belonged to for the time. Other good men have been "prisoners in the Lord." Judson lay in prison twenty-two months in Burmah but when they finally let him out he did not want to leave Burmah, neither did he hate the folks who imprisoned him. John Bunyan was in prison twelve years because he preached the gospel; and when they offered to let him out if he would promise not to preach any more, he said: "Though the moss grow on my eyelids, I would not make such a promise." Yes, God will let His folks who serve Him faithfully lie in prison and sometimes die there, or be burned, or eaten by wild beasts, but He will comfort and keep them and give them reward and blessing and glory forever in that great day.

We have said this much about Paul as a prisoner in order to ask the reader to remember that it is God's man suffering in prison who is here asking us to live worthily of our Christian calling. Hear these words from the heart of a hero, sounding out of a prison clear and strong as a silver bell: "I the prisoner in the Lord beseech, admonish, you to walk worthily of the calling wherewith you were called."

Before we talk about the "calling" let us say that it is a mistake to call the first three chapters of Ephesians the "doctrinal" section and the last three the "practical" part. No such idea existed in Paul's mind. He never divorced doctrine from practice, or practice from doctrine. One doubts whether he ever even thought of any distinction between God's eternal grace in the heart and God's grace enacted, exemplified in the life. There is more said about Christian conduct in the latter chapters and more about grace in the first ones, but grace undergirds everything in the last part of the book and Christian behavior is assumed and implied and at times stated in all the first portion.

In the beginning of his doctrine the author gets no further than the fourth verse of chapter one when he blazons forth one of his most practical statements about holy living—"according as He chose us in Him before the foundation of the world that we *should be holy and* without blame before Him." Holiness, without the eternal purpose and activity on God's part is impossible. A blameless life as the results of God's activity is inevitable. In that sentence he unites doctrine and practice for all time to come. In the first sentence of the practical section (4:1) he yokes them together again with, "I the prisoner in the Lord beseech you to walk worthily of the calling" (your eternal choice or election by God) wherewith ye were called. The Call of God has become effectual in your case through the Word and by the Spirit, he would say to them, now you work out and effectuate God's eternal purpose by your blameless behavior as God's chosen ones. What could be more practical than "walk worthily" or more doctrinal and deeply mystical than "the Calling wherewith ye were called?"

In the second chapter Paul snaps out doctrine in short dynamic sentences: "For by grace have you been saved through faith, and that not of you, the gift of God, not of works, that no one should boast." The explanation, the very counterpart of that great statement about our salvation is: "For we are his handiwork created in Christ Jesus for good works, which God prepared before hand that we should walk in them." We "who have been saved" (Paul used a perfect passive tense) are His handiwork and were created in Christ Jesus for the very purpose of good works, and God prepared the good works beforehand. He created us in Christ so that we could do the works he had mapped out for us. The plan of our life and behavior are just as truly a part of the divine purpose as is our salvation. If we fail in performance we shall be chastized in His own way, and we shall miss much in reward in the future life that He wants to give us. He said of David and his seed: "If his children forsake my law, And walk not in mine ordinances,

> If they break my statutes
> And keep not my Commandments
> Then will I visit their transgression with the rod
> And their iniquity with stripes,
> But my loving kindness will I not utterly take from him
> Nor suffer my faithfulness to fail."

One believes that He will be just as true to those under the covenant of grace as He was to those under the law.

Doctrine was as native to Paul as exhaling his breath, and practical exhortation to godliness was as natural as drawing air into his lungs. He could no more preach one without the other than he could walk on one foot. He knew they must go *"pari passu."* He knew the bony framework of the body cannot live and do its work without blood, muscle, sinew, and flesh to clothe it, also that the fleshly trappings of the body can get nowhere without the bony skeleton to carry it. He was the best balanced, most equi-poised and sober-minded man of all time. He had more common sense, and more tempered zeal with knowledge to control it, more holy fire without fanaticism to explode it, more evangelistic fervor with doctrinal stamina to undergird it, than ten thousand of his critics who talk of his "epilepsy" and his "schizophrenia," and think he was a case for their psycho-analysis. He held the mystery of Christ in a pure con-science, illustrated it in a life of complete devotion, and spoke it in a modulated language of sound speech as no other interpreter of his Lord has been able to do.

Paul urges a godly life upon his readers by an appeal to their mystical experience: "Walk worthily of the calling wherewith ye were called." The divine Call, the eternal election of grace wherewith God had claimed them has been made effectual now in their experience, and they are urged with argument as high as infinity and tender as a heart throb to translate that experience into daily conduct. What is the calling but the eternal choice of God, based on His elective purpose, effectuated in His appealing to the human spirit to come out and find rest in Jesus? What but the thunderous warning that death lurks by the sinner's way? What is it but the prevenient grace of God that inclines the will, con-vinces the judgment, convicts the conscience, and brings one by the word and through the blessed Spirit into an experimental knowledge of the Redeemer?

With Paul the calling is not a mere sound, not a stentorian proclamation, not solely a polite and gracious invitation. It is God's choice of His people with an in-vitation so revealingly personal, so sweetly insistent, and so cogently presented that the invited one gladly accepts it and comes to the feast.

Someone says: "Suppose God called and the soul did not come?" To be sure the gospel gives an invitation which many decline, but there is something deeper here. It is an act as well as an invitation. It is the eternal choice of God actuated in our experience. There is a release of divine energy in the soul which conquers by love's authority. God has manifold and mighty ways of bringing men to acceptance of the truth. The truth which is received, the divine call which is accepted and becomes an experience in the heart is to be wrought out in the life. "I the prisoner in the Lord beseech you" by this experience which you have to live worthily of the source, power and blessing of the experience.

An expression of this walk will be lowly mindedness. Christians, of all men, should not be conceited or vainglorious. Egotism is a besetting sin of multitudes of the royal family, including many preachers. Dr. William E. Hatcher and Dr. A. E. Owen of Virginia were life long friends. Dr. Owen had a pompous, conceited bearing, though underneath there was a true, golden heart. One day somebody said to Dr. Hatcher: "Don't you think that young man Owen is very conceited?" Hatcher replied: "Well, I don't know that he is any more so than you and I are, but he can't keep from showing it as we can." How charming and mighty it is to be lowly-minded; not weak minded; not subservient or grovelling; but humble, reasonable, with mental poise and fairness of opinion and judgment about oneself and concerning others. To be firm as a rock in conviction but as responsive to truth and mercy as an Aeolian harp is to catch the wind and convert it into music to soothe aching ears.

Moses was surpassingly great largely because he was the meekest man on earth. He was long suffering. How otherwise could he have endured his troubles and the criticism of Israel? The Greek word for long suffering means "big spirited," "big minded." What a trial to human patience, and maybe to divine, is the little, pesky, pestiferous minded man who does not know the difference in a mouse and a mastodon, in a gnat and a giant, in a notion and a conviction! Meekness is M-I-G-H-T,

and not m-i-t-e. Robert E. Lee was so meek and merciful that he picked up a young bird that had fallen from
the nest and placed it back under its mother. But Lee
was a veritable Jove in battle. John A. Broadus was
meek, but was an awful scourge to chastise hypocrisy
and dishonesty. The one who was "meek and lowly in
heart" so goaded the Pharisees for their duplicity that
they determined to kill him.

If there is lowly mindedness, meekness and long suffering in the spirit, the injunction "forbearing one another in love" will become not only a possibility but a
pleasure as well. Paul's word for forbearing means
"holding yourselves back" from one another. People
of the same church family often set on one another
with tooth and claw to rend and devour each other in
the spirit of ravenous beasts.

To walk worthily of our heavenly calling there are
both subjective and objective requirements, that is, certain conditions or states of mind and heart that must
be in us, and certain spiritual activities and efforts in
which we must engage. Lowly mindedness, meekness,
long suffering, constitute an inward triad which must
reign in queenly beauty and power.

No one can adorn the Christian calling without having
those very heart qualities that were completely regnant
in the soul of Jesus. Then there are objective or outward activities and characteristics which must rule our
conduct. Paul gives two of them here—"holding yourselves back from one another in love," and "zealously
striving to guard the unity of the Spirit in the bond
of peace."

As an explication of this injunction to guard the unity
of the Spirit he says, "One body and one Spirit just as
ye were called in one hope of your calling: one Lord,

one faith, one baptism, and one God and Father of
all who is over all, through all and in you all." There
is one calling or salvation to each child of God (and he
is writing to Christians, not sinners) and one Spirit who
brings it about; there is or will be one body of Christ
consisting of all the saved in all time, who will be the
general assembly and Church of the First Born whose
names are written in heaven. The church on earth,
called His body, is a type of the general Church in glory.
There is one lord who made one offering for sin, who
trod the winepress alone, who is the image of the invisible God, who was the first born of all creation; and
He is before all things and in him all things hold together; and He is the head of the body, the church.
There is only one faith in this one Lord. There are
not various kinds of faith. Faith means implicit, peace-
ful trust in Christ.

There is one water baptism and Paul is speaking of
that here. That means baptized one time. It has nothing
to do with modes of baptism, or immersion as contrasted
with sprinkling and pouring. Modes of baptism were
not heard of for two or three hundred years after Paul
wrote that. There is no such thing as modes of baptism.
It's carrying coals to New Castle to talk of "baptism
by immersion." You had as well say "baptism by baptism." Why the pleonasm? Immersion by a New Testament church of a true believer in the name of the Trinity
is baptism. It is called a burial also (Rom. 6:4, Col. 2:12).
It is impossible to bury by sprinkling or pouring. The
Greek word "rantizo" means to sprinkle, and the Greek
word "cheo" means to pour, but they are NEVER used in
connection with baptism. Those who have faith in Christ
should be baptized one time in keeping with the unity
of the Spirit, the unity of the body of Christ, the church,

the unity of the faith. Then he traces it back to mono-
theism, "one God and Father of all who is over all and
through all and in all." There is one faith in the Lord,
there is one body of the one Lord, and one baptism
symbolizing His death and our faith in the one Lord
whom we accepted when we died to sin, and rose to a
new life in Christ, who conquered death and the grave
and will in due time redeem our bodies from the dust.

Paul's doctrine of unity of the many in one body
does not destroy the identity and the duty of the individual. It does not encourage the idleness and the
irresponsibility of one or of some who would let others
do the work. The unity does not make all have the
same talents or assign them to the same work. "But to
each one of us grace was given according to the measure
of the gift of Christ." His grace is free and His bestow-
ment of it absolutely sovereign. If another has more
sense than I there is no place for envy on my part. If
I have more than another, there is no occasion for
glorying.

It is disappointing to find a current scholar who under-
stands "Gave gifts to men" to mean that the several
ministerial groups mentioned in chapter four-eleven
were gifts to the "universal church." It may be said
that first, as stated in another chapter of this book,
"universal church" is neither a phrase nor an idea to be
found in the New Testament. Why emphasize "Gifts
to *men*," or mankind to try to "get over" the idea that
the ministerial groups were given to a "universal church"
for mankind rather than to the local church? Why
couldn't these ministerial groups be gifts to mankind
through the local church as well as—even much better
than—they could be gifts to men through an invisible
church—which is not a New Testament concept. *God's*

Gifts to the Churches by Mrs. Ruth Carver Gardner gives the correct interpretation of this passage in excellent form.

The local church at Philippi had pastors and deacons. The Jerusalem church had an Evangelist in Philip. If Luke is correct in his report (Acts 20:17), the church at Ephesus had Elders, who are generally regarded as the same as bishops and pastors. At any rate, they were officers in a local, not a universal, church. The Lord commanded that in case brethren at variance could not be reconciled the matter should be brought to the church. It would seem difficult to bring a matter to a "universal church," which does not exist, or to the church the whole body of Christ which is known to nobody but God: and which will never be assembled until it meets in the consummated kingdom of heaven.

Paul says: "And He gave some apostles (as apostles, or to be apostles); and some prophets; and some evangelists; and some pastors and teachers." There are four groups enumerated. Apostles, prophets, evangelists, and pastor and teachers. It is perfectly plain from the Greek Construction that there are four groups, and that the fourth group consists of pastors and teachers, not that the pastors were different persons from the teachers, but that the pastor was a teacher also and the teacher was a pastor. It was the same man doing the work of the shepherd and the work of the instructor of the flock.

One has read two authors who advanced the idea that the evangelist was an understudy, so to speak, of the pastor; one suggesting that he was like a city missionary working in the suburbs and outlying areas as a helper of the city pastor. If anyone will study Paul's Greek carefully, he will see that the apostle sets out four groups plainly, orderly, without any implication of superiority or inferiority. They all seem to be independent and equal in their own sphere according to Paul's statement.

"Apostles" does not mean the twelve apostles exclusively, but men of the apostolic character, not only like the twelve, but men like Barnabas, Stephen, and James, who was pastor at Jerusalem—men of apostolic type, faithfulness and ability. Prophets were both foretellers and forthtellers. They sometimes revealed future events. They sometimes spoke forth the truth of God to men and pointed out the way in which men should walk.

The evangelist was a teller of good news, as the word itself signifies, specifically, of course, to bring men into reconciliation with God. Timothy was commanded to "do the work of an evangelist." Bringing men to Christ is the first work. Without that, Christianity is not propagated, churches are not founded, the body of Christ is not growing.

Pastors and teachers were the shepherds and teachers of the church. How anyone can think that those functions can be carried on by a "universal church" which is not organized and not local in character and operation is extremely mysterious.

Christ gave His command to disciple, baptize, and teach all nations to a definite, visible group that He had taught and trained; a group who were bound by the law of fellowship and service; a group that He must have had in mind when He said "Tell it to the church." To be sure it is the duty of every Christian, of whatever name or denomination to do what he can to bring in the kingdom of God, but the fact remains if the New Testament makes sense, that the Lord ordained, constituted, and appointed His church as His agent for preaching His gospel to all men. And "church" in the New Testament never means a "convention," "convocation," "Synod," "Conference," or an aggregation of congregations bound together by ecclesiastical or canon law, which is ruled by priestly authority. "Church" in New Testament usage nearly always refers to a local congregation and when there is more than one, it is "churches."

The apostle then brings in here what might at first seem an irrelevant passage, a quotation. "He saith, having ascended on high He led Captivity Captive (captured captivity, conquered the conqueror, killed the killer) and gave gifts to men." And he proceeds to interpret the quotation: "Now this, what is it that He ascended but that He also descended into the lower parts of the earth." But we vainly wish that in his interpretation he might have told us just what "the lower parts of the earth" means. Was it into hades to preach to the spirits in prison? Into the grave where he lay three days and nights? Or more simply, and, one thinks, more in harmony with his purpose and his context, "unto the earth" on his mission, that is, he had to come to the world on His redemptive mission before He could go back to the Father. In "lower parts of the earth," "of the earth" can be an appositional Genitive, translated "lower parts which is the earth." This is a much more natural interpretation in the light of the next statement. "He that descended is also the one who ascended." His coming was significant because He came from the Father to do the Father's will; and His going away was full of meaning because He did the Father's will, and then returned to the right hand of God to administer His kingdom.

The Mending of the Saints

"And He gave some as apostles, and some prophets, and some evangelists, and some pastors and teachers unto (with a view to, or purpose) the mending (or equipment) of the saints unto the work of ministering (or service) for the building up of the body of Christ." "For the perfecting of the saints" is not a happy translation. The word does not mean moral perfection, or perfection as completion of growth in the sense of full grown. It is the word used where they were "mending their nets" (Matt. 4:21). The idea is to "repair, recondition," or "mend," "equip." How much the saints do need mending every pastor knows as he lies on his bed in the small hours and prays that Jane may master a tattling tongue, that Mary may quell a tempestuous temper, that Tom shall not give in to greed, that Luther may be steadfast and not unstable, that banker Jones may buy up the opportunity knowing what the will of the Lord is, as readily as he buys rising stocks understanding what the profits will be. When temptation assails, and sometimes soils; when sorrow falls upon hearts that are broken, and reverses of fortune, and disappointments in children, and breaks in the marriage bond come, how much the saints need mending.

There is a fine touch here that a wrong translation of the King James Version may have caused the English reader to miss. Paul did not say "for the work of *the* ministry." He said: "For work of ministering," or "for the work of ministering," that is, "serving." The word for "work" does not have the definite article but we may supply it because of the following Genitive case which makes "work" definite. What Paul says is that the work of apostles, prophets, evangelists, pastors and teachers is to preach the gospel, win the lost to Christ, shepherd the sheep, mend the saints and prepare them for service, for the blessed work of building up and bringing to perfection the whole body of Christ, the church of God. Leaders are to develop and train the church, and the church is to do the work of serving. Then he goes on to show what the joyful result will be: "Until the time when we all shall arrive at the unity of the faith, and of the accurate knowledge of the Son of God, unto a completed, or mature man, unto the measure of the statue of the fulness of Christ." Try to imagine what it would mean for this sinful world if all God's people should come to the unity of the faith and of the accurate knowledge of the Son of God. Unity can be attained only by accurate knowledge of God. Paul gives us the result of such unity of the faith and knowledge in chapter 4:14-16: "So that no longer we may be children tossed about and borne around like a whirlpool by every wind of teaching in the deceit, or dishonesty, of men (The word means dice throwing. They loaded the dice in Paul's days as in ours—the same old gambler's trick) in craftiness for the machination of error, but 'truthing' it in love we may grow up in Him in all things who is the head, Christ." "Truthing it" in love is literally his word. That does not only mean "speaking the truth," it means being the truth. As the Negro preacher said: "The truth has two parts, believing it and *behaving* it."

This arrangement is all of divine appointment. Paul says with emphasis, "and He *Himself* gave some apostles, some prophets," etc. The different ministerial functions are fixed by the Lord Himself. Some specially talented men like Paul, and Spurgeon, and Carey, and Broadus may do several things with success and distinction, yet God meant that there shall be special lines of work done by different men. Also that grace and talent and equipment are given according to the measure of the gift of Christ. And again all these gifts and all ministerial functions are gifts to the churches for their appreciation and for their edification in Christian service and growth in Christian character, until the saints reach a full grown stature like unto the stature of the fulness of Christ. The outcome is "the head is Christ from whom the whole body harmoniously joined and knit together through every joint of supply according to an efficiency in the measure of each one of the parts of the body makes increase (growth) of itself for building itself up in love."

General Statement of Christian Conduct

In chapter 4:17-24 the apostle states in a general or abstract way, the principle of good behavior. "This therefore I say and testify in the Lord that ye walk no longer even as the Gentiles walk in the vanity of their mind, being darkened in their thoughts, alienated from the life of God, because of the ignorance which is in them, on account of the hardening of their heart, who being such as are passed feeling gave themselves over to lasciviousness to work all uncleanness with greediness. But ye did not so learn Christ, if, as I assume, ye heard him and were taught in him even as the truth is in Jesus that ye put off concerning the former manner of life the old man which is growing more corrupt according to the lust of deceit, and be renewed in the spirit of your mind and put on the new man which according to God was created in righteousness and holiness of the truth." That is not hard to understand. It is plain enough. The difficulty is in the doing of it. But it is well to state the truth in general and universal terms. That convinces the judgment and wins the assent of every right thinking person. Moreover, the general statement does not provoke opposition, but preaching in platitudes is not enough. Paul never stopped there. When he comes to his next paragraph and tells them to quit lying, the fire may fly. However, it is a wise approach to win assent to the truth in principle. They knew they should not live as the Gentiles. Some of them were Gentiles who had found freedom in Christ and achieved victory over their former manner of life. They knew Gentiles walked in the vanity of their mind, were darkened in their thoughts, alienated from the life of God because of their ignorance which resulted from their wilful hardening of their hearts. They were past feeling and did not care, therefore gave rein to their lusts and to every uncleanness and did it with eager abandon to unchastity. That is not the way for God's servants. They did not so learn Christ. They have put off their former behavior and ditched the old man that is growing more putrid daily. The called ones have been renewed in the spirit of their mind. That must mean the spiritual and best moral quality of their mind, rather a newly created mind and conscience and will, which distinguishes them as a spiritual entity distinct from, and greater than, mere intellectuality or mental ability. Mr. Spurgeon held that the unsaved man is only intellectual or soul and that the "spirit" is a creation of the new birth. One can hardly go with him there, but surely man considered mentally is not the same as when considered as spirit, or spiritual. The saints have been renewed in the deepest depths of their being and have put on the new man, the new life, which was created according to the being and power of God in righteousness and holiness of the truth.

In the next paragraph which reaches from 4:25 to 5:14, Paul goes into particulars and gives many concrete practical exhortations. On which account, because you have put on the new man, because you have been created according to God in righteousness and holiness of the truth "put away falsehood." It is more than "lying." It is false being, false intimations, looks and desires— everything false and deceptive in word, deed and desire; and begin right now to speak and keep on speaking the truth every one with his neighbor, because we (all Christians) are members of one another.

Without giving full, accurate translation here, let us note hurriedly the many exhortations and statements in this paragraph. 1. Put away falsehood. 2. Speak the truth. 3. Be angry. 4. Don't sin. 5. Don't let the sun set on your wrath. 6. Don't give place to the devil. 7. Quit stealing. 8. Toil and work with your hands to have something to give to the needy. 9. Let no "rotten" word come out of your mouth. 10. Speak for edification; to give grace to your hearers. 11. Don't grieve the Holy Spirit. 12. Ye were sealed by the Spirit unto the day of redemption. 13. Put away all bitterness, anger, wrath, uproar, blasphemy, and wickedness. 14. Be kind. 15. Be tender hearted. 16. Be forgiving, because Christ forgave you. 17. Be imitators of God. 18. Walk in love. 19. Christ loved you. 20. He gave Himself up as a sacrifice in your behalf, as your substitute. 21. Don't let forni- cation, uncleanness, and covetousness be even named among you. 22. Baseness, foolish talking or low jesting put away. 23. You well know that every fornicator, unclean person, and covetous one who is an idolater has no inheritance in God's kingdom. 24. Don't be deceived by empty words for because of these things God's wrath comes on the children of disobedience. 25. Don't be partakers with them. 26. You were once darkness. 27. You are now light in the Lord. 28. Walk as children of light. 29. The fruit of the light is goodness, justice, and truth. 30. They prove what is pleasing to the Lord. 31. Have no fellowship with fruitless works of darkness. 34. Things reproved by the light are made manifest, exposed. 35. Let sleepers awake and rise up from the dead. 36. If you do this, Christ will shine upon you. What a pity that we preachers can find nothing to preach!

A few statements in this plethoric paragraph require some comment. We have spoken of "putting away falsehood." Now notice the strange and difficult command: "Be ye angry and sin not." Dr. Robertson calls "be ye angry" a "permissive imperative." Says it is not a command. The words are taken from Psalms 4:4 and follow the Septuagint, the Greek version of the Old Testament. Some translate the Hebrew text "tremble and sin not"—Ex. Greek Testament. There is a use of the imperative which assumes a thing as true without commanding it. That would probably meet Dr. Robertson's idea of a "permissive imperative." The Expositor's Greek Testament says the wording of this text does not admit of a "permissive imperative" because there is no adversative word, or disjunctive, attached to the second member of the sentence. One believes that is true, and that it is not a permissive imperative but that "as used by Paul here, the words recognize the fact that anger has its rightful place and may be a duty, while they indicate how easily it may pass into the sinful"—Ex.G.T.

One who could pass along the street and see a big hulk of a man choking and beating a little boy to death and not get mad would not be much like Christ. Those who can, with equanimity, see white-slave traffickers decoying innocent unsuspecting girls into a life of shame worse than death, are little better than the scoundrels who perpetrate such deeds. One thinks Paul would say: "Be angry, and do something about it, but don't become a prey of your indignation and commit murder or sin." Anger turned loose, running riot, gone to stark madness and uncontrollable fury would destroy anyone's power to right the wrongs, and would also cause him to sin.

Don't let the sun go down upon your wrath is wise counsel. Better not sleep over our misunderstandings and harsh words. They will harden into grievances, and grievances require no trained nurse to keep them alive. Wives and husbands who go to sleep with malice in their hearts toward each other are on the way to divorce courts. Cherishing malice gives the devil his supreme opportunity.

Let one who is stealing quit stealing and go to work, and become a helper of others instead of a purloiner of the property of others. Laziness coupled with covetousness makes thieves. Those who will not work have no right to eat. They should have the privilege of starving. That needs to be said in the world today as never before. Society needs helpmeets, not deadbeats.

"Let no rotten word proceed out of your mouth"— Paul's word means "rotten." "Mouth" is singular but the Greek word for "your" is plural. It applies to all. We expect cleanliness of speech of preachers and of women, and have a right to expect it from all Christians. Sad to say, we are sometimes disappointed. Sometimes thoughtless laymen embarrass ministers by telling them off color stories. A good thing for the preacher to do in such case is to have his attention attracted to something out yonder and go to see about it and leave the impudent storyteller minus an audience.

Immediately following this proscription of rotten words, Paul says: "and do not grieve the Holy Spirit of God by whom ye were sealed unto the day of redemption." As logical a writer as Paul did not accidentally drop that injunction in right after the remark about corrupt words. "Grieve not the Holy Spirit" may be taken as a general, universal, and timely command, but Paul was no doubt making a particular application of it here. He knew, and we know, that minds in which filthy words dwell will find no place for the Spirit of God. Tongues that are lathered with filthy speech cannot be tuned to intone the melodies inspired by the Holy Spirit. An example comes to mind of a preacher in years agone. He was a talented man, of brilliant mind and ready speech. He was educationally trained. He had good pastorates, also denominational positions of great influence. He was keen in controversy, versatile in phrase, and quick and clever in wit, which entertained and drew people to him. But he had an unclean mouth, and he was without spiritual power to minister to the deepest needs of men's souls.

Carrying forward his thought the apostle says: "Be ye therefore imitators of God as beloved children; and walk in love, even as Christ also loved you, and gave Himself up for us, an offering and a sacrifice to God for an odor of a sweet smell" (5:1.2).

"Imitators of God!" God in Christ Jesus is the only adequate ideal for the Christian life. We are commanded to love even as Christ loved us; and His love for us eventuated in His offering Himself as a sacrifice to God. His was not an accidental death. It pleased God to bruise Him. There are three persons or parties gravely and greatly concerned in the atonement, viz; the eternal Father pouring out His suffering love in the gift of His Son, the obedient Son meekly bowing His thorn-crowned head and gripping the accursed nails that held Him to a cross, and the condemned sinner who is forgiven all when he looks to Him who hung on the tree.

Paul says that this sacrifice is well pleasing unto God. The bold figure "for an odor of a sweet smell" is distasteful to some supercilious, fastidious souls. It was, however, pleasing to God; and was good enough for Paul who had seen and talked with Jesus in a heavenly vision, and been apprehended by the risen Lord from a violent life and constrained to a course of sacrificial service to God and men. We shall not go wrong if we let a man of such experiences point out the way of salvation which is the way of The Cross.

XII

GRACE MASTER IN ALL RELATIONS

Ephesians 5:15-6:24

While on a city bus one heard the operator say to an elderly woman who was getting off: "Now watch your step." That is what Paul says here (5:15) with a snappy imperative: "Look therefore sharply how you walk, not as foolish but as wise, buying up the opportunity because the days are evil. On this account do not be stupid, but understand what the will of the Lord is. And don't be drunk with wine (and if you have the habit quit it right now) wherein is riot, but be filled with the Spirit, speaking unto yourselves in psalms, and hymns, and spiritual songs, singing and making melody in your heart to the Lord, giving thanks for all things (that are right and good) to God, even the Father in the name of our Lord Jesus Christ."

Good conduct does not just happen. It is studied, thoughtful and purposeful. Being truly Christian is not caught by accident like the measles. If we do not work at it, there will be no results. Those who do not watch where they are going will soon be in the ditch. Better look ahead. The long look is of supreme value. Spiritual myopia, near sightedness, is fatal to Christian living. Peter (11 Pet. 1:9) says: "For he that lacketh these things is blind (myopia) seeing only what is near, having forgotten the cleansing from his old sins." If we keep our "eyes skinned" to detect evil as well as good Satan will not slip up on the blind side of us when he appears as an angel of light. We shall discover his approach from afar. This is the part of wisdom. Anything else is folly which will vitiate all behavior and destroy all Christian influence.

Paul has an important word here about opportune service in an evil day. "Buying up the season, making use of the occasion, or grasping the opportunity" is his thought. Then he gives as a reason: "because the days are evil." Talk about quitting because the going is hard? Absurd! Leave the field on account of opposition! "But I will tarry at Ephesus until Pentecost, for a great door and effectual is opened unto me, *and there* are *many adversaries*" (1 Cor. 16: 9-10) is his answer. That conjunctive conjunction, "and," is a battle cry. Cowards say: "Yes, there are great opportunities, *but* there are so many difficulties you can't accomplish anything." This old warrior says: "Let the Lord and me get at those adversaries and see what happens." The difficulties were music in his ears like the sound of the starting gong to the eager race horse that is "rearing to go." He wanted to preach where the gospel had not been preached. Where there are more sinners God can win more saints. Where the greatest darkness reigns the light is worth the most. Where there is more sickness, and sorrow, and suffering, and death, there more, and better, physicians must go to minister and heal. Ignorance is a Macedonian cry for "the light of the knowledge of the glory of God in the face of Jesus Christ" (11 Cor. 4:6). Where world conditions are the worst, the saving gospel of the miraculous, Virgin-born Son of God can do its best. When the "gospel" of Communism fares forth in fury to sabotage and liquidate the social order and subjugate the world to its god of nationalism, the

God and Father of our Lord Jesus Christ can defeat this god of clay by the blood of the cross and the word of testimony of His servants.

The world is in flux and formative period. It is like the concrete that will harden in the mass in a few hours if it is not poured in the forms to make the mighty bridge. It is like the iron in glowing white heat which the smith must hammer now or never. If Southern Baptists knew and cared about the world-wide opportunity for gospel conquest they would put nine thousand foreign missionaries on the field instead of nine hundred; and that number would be vastly increased as other fields could be opened and equipment secured and organization perfected for assimilating more workers. One thinks God is trying to get the ears of His churches to say to them that this is the day of opportunity and destiny when crucified-living and courageous conflict can win the war and put Christ on the throne.

The very extremes of conduct oppose each other: "Be not drunk with wine wherein is riot, but be filled with the Spirit." This is an apt illustration because of the extreme unlikeness of the two things compared, except in one respect. No two states could be more unlike than drunkenness and the being filled with the Holy Spirit. But in one respect they are alike. They both master and control the one they possess. When liquor is in, wits are out. The drunken man is under complete dominance of rum. His tongue and temper are motivated by Satan. The Spirit filled man is under the power of God. He is the mouth piece through which God can speak, the medium through which divine power can flow. Godless ones looked on the disciples at Pentecost and said: "They are filled with new wine." Not because they behaved as drunken men, but because they were possessed by some mighty power which the un-circumcized in heart could not understand.

The Spirit's presence will turn the life to song. Psalms and hymns and spiritual songs burst forth when He rules in the spirit and the heart is filled with melody unto the Lord, and with thankfulness unto God. Another result is that those who are filled with the Spirit "submit themselves to one another in the fear of Christ." This is an outward, visible effect which all may see, of the inward state. This does not mean the surrender of freedom and personality, but love and respect and consideration for one another, and cooperation with and service to one another in holy fear of the Lord Jesus.

> "Till David touched his sacred lyre,
> In silence lay the unbreathing wire,
> But when he swept its chords along,
> Even angels stooped to hear the song,
> So sleeps the soul till Thou O Lord,
> Shalt deign to touch its lifeless chord—
> When waked by Thee, its breath shall rise
> In music worthy of the skies."

From the deeply spiritual exhortations unto Christian behavior in the first of this long paragraph Paul moves on without even a paragraph break to the matter of domestic relations. "Wives submit yourselves to your own husbands as unto the Lord, for a man is head of the (his) wife as also Christ is head of the church; He Himself is saviour of the body, (the church). Nevertheless as the Church is subject to Christ, so likewise also let the wives be subject to their husbands in everything. Husbands, love your wives even as also Christ loved the Church and delivered Himself up in its behalf, in order that He might sanctify it having cleansed it in the bath of the water with the word, in order that He might present it to Himself a glorious Church, not having spot or wrinkle or any such thing but that it might be holy and blameless. So ought also the husbands to love their own wives as their own bodies. He who loves his own wife loves himself, for nobody ever hated his own flesh, but nourishes and cherishes it, even as also Christ the Church, for we are members of His body. For this cause a man shall leave (future tense with ethical intent, what should be) his father and his mother and cleave unto his wife and the two shall be one flesh. This mystery is great but I speak with reference to Christ and to the Church. Nevertheless let you each one so love his own wife as himself, and the wife see that she reverences her husband." The above is the reading of Chapter 5:22-33.

This passage has been the occasion, though not the cause, of endless furor concerning women's marital status. Has not this contention come from reading and considering only one side of the marriage obligation at a time to the exclusion of the other side? A wife says: "I am not going to be obedient to any man." Wait a minute, dear sister. Suppose that man loves you as Christ loved the Church. Suppose he is willing to die on a cross or be consumed in fire to protect your honor, promote your happiness, clothe your body, and nourish your soul? Would it be hard to submit yourself to a man like that? This is the sort of man Paul expects you to obey. Now Mr. Husband puts in a complaint, saying: "My wife pays no attention to the Scriptural command to obey me." But, husband, have you made that woman know that you love her well enough to die for her? Paul had the greatest appreciation of good women, and was the greatest helper of women of all the men of

Biblical times, so far as the record shows. He had no desire to enslave women, and no purpose to pamper the conceit of men. He saw the ruin in heathen homes and in heathen society caused by the insubordination of wives to their husbands. He knew the libidinous conduct of both husbands and wives which resulted in that heathen society from the loosening of the marriage bond. He also knew that if a husband loves "his own wife" (he repeats that phrase) as Christ loves the Church and the wife has a holy reverence for her husband, nothing on earth or from the pit can separate them. He knew that sort of home would rear children in the nurture and admonition of the Lord.

We know little or nothing about Paul's home life. I think he had been married. He said he gave his vote against the Christians so he must have been a member of the Sanhedrin and only married men could have membership in that body. He never mentions his father or mother or a wife, but my guess would be that he had had a wife whom he had loved as devotedly as one heart ever loved another, and that he had lost her by death, or possible desertion when he became a Christian. There seems to me to be a heart throb, a note of sadness in his statement that he counted "all loss for Christ." He may have been thinking of Ruth, or Lois, or Miriam who walked no longer by his side when he followed the Nazarene. Surmise? Maybe so, but to me it helps to explain some things in his wonderful teaching here and in Corinthians about the marriage relation. If the things he says here about husbands and wives could be realized, divorce courts would die of starvation and Christian homes would be such heavens on earth that folks would feel quite at home when they go up to the heavenly mansions.

His injunction to children to obey their parents that they may be long on the earth, because obedience to parents is the first commandment with a promise, and his command to fathers not to provoke their children to wrath but bring them up in the nurture and admonition of the Lord, speak the last word on pedagogy.

Agitators and reformers have attacked Paul concerning his teaching to slaves. But we know that many of these early Christians were slaves. That may explain their night time meetings. They met all night at Troas when Paul preached most of the night. They met for prayer all night when Peter was delivered from prison. The slave Christians were driven all day at their task by cruel masters and went to worship at night. If they had been incited to insurrection by fanatical anti-slavery teaching, thousands of them would have had their heads chopped off instantly. There was not a ghost of a chance for successful revolution against their masters, or against slavery at that time. Paul would have been an unpardonable fool to have blurted out some wild pronouncements against slave holders which could only have brought death to many, and increased suffering to all the slave Christians. But don't think this master of social ethics failed to put a noose around the neck of slavery and start it on its way to the gallows. He planted some TNT under that accursed custom which resulted in blowing it to atoms. He cautioned the slaves to be obedient, "not according to eyeservice as men pleasers but as servants of Christ doing the will of God out of the soul." Then he proceeded to plant the bomb: "And ye masters, do the same things unto them (your slaves) leaving off threatening, knowing that both their and your Lord is in heaven and there is no respect of persons with Him." They were "kurioi" or masters, or bosses. But the real

"Kurios" (with capital) or Lord, is in heaven. He puts "their Lord" first, a pretty broad hint that He will avenge and vindicate them. And he is "your Lord also." The same Lord who judges these innocent and helpless ones that you may wrong will also judge you who have done the wrong. The Lord who bears these up in fortitude and friendship under your tortures and saves them unto His heavenly kingdom can forgive your wrongs and make you a brother beloved of these whom you manhandle as goods and cattles. Personality is precious and sacrosanct in the sight of God and there is no respect of persons with Him. You call these "slaves" but they are God's freed men. You think you are free but God sees you as a slave of sin which is hurrying you to His impartial judgment throne. In a society where personality is more precious than all worldly treasure everybody is somebody and nobody can be everybody.

Paul followed the same course when he sent Onesimus, the runaway slave, whom he had fished out of some pond of iniquity in Rome and led to Christ, back to Philemon, the master of Onesimus. The teaching there is that Onesimus is Philemon's property, but he is now his brother in the Lord. He was once "unprofitable, but now he is profitable to thee and to me." "I want to be very courteous about it, Philemon," Paul would say, "but you remember you owe your own salvation to me under the Lord, and I know your big heart and know that you are going to do more than I ask in sending Onesimus back to me here in Rome where I am suffering for the dear Lord we all love. Meanwhile, Philemon, tell Apphia to get the prophets' chamber ready, for I will be released from this imprisonment and I am coming to Colossae to see you and Apphia and

Archippus, and we will invite the whole church to come in some night after their day's toil, and I will tell them about my stay in Rome, and about the noble Roman Christians." That is the kind of teaching that exploded slavery. Those who would classify Paul as an apologizer for slavery know nothing of the spirit and genius of the man.

After giving the many weighty counsels about conduct, the marriage relation, bringing up children, the behavior of slaves toward their masters and duties of masters to their slaves, the apostle sets out the equipment necessary for Christians that they may meet his requirement.

"In respect to the rest (6:10-20) be made (passive voice) strong (be powerful) in the Lord and in the conquering strength of his might. Put on the whole armor of God in order that you may be able to stand against the wiles of the devil; for our wrestling is not against blood and flesh, but against rulerships, against authorities, against the world rulers of this darkness, against the spiritual forces of wickedness in the heavenly (or high) places. Wherefore take up the whole armor of God, in order that ye may be able to withstand in the evil day and having done all to stand. Stand therefore, being girt about your loin with truth and having on the breast plate of righteousness, and (sandals) bound underneath the feet with the preparation of the gospel of peace, in all things taking the shield of faith, by which ye shall be able to quench all the fiery darts of the wicked; and take the helmet of salvation and the sword of the Spirit, which is the word of God, through all prayer and supplication, and watching thereunto with all perseverance and supplication concerning all the saints, and in my behalf, so that utterance in opening my mouth may be given to me to make known with boldness, (or freedom of speech) the mystery of the gospel in behalf of which I am an ambassador in a chain, in order that in it I may be bold to speak as I ought to speak."

Paul frequently used the imagery of war for illustration. He had seen Roman soldiers from his boyhood. Here he follows, in the main though not completely, the equipment of a soldier as given by Polybius. It consisted of shield, sword, lance, helmet, greaves, and breastplate. Then the soldier was fully armed, or panoplied. This armor protected the most vital parts. The shield would ward off strokes as well as protect the body from them. The sword was deadly for close combat, and the spear or javelin could be thrown to fell an enemy at a distance. The helmet resisted a sword thrust, while greaves and breastplate covered the legs and the chest. Paul adds "the girdle of truth." Anyone's loins are stronger with a good tight girdle. Truth is a supreme power in all spiritual conflict, and righteousness gives one "the strength of ten because his heart is pure." The sandals of peace makes the gospel messenger fleet of foot and sure of his footing, while the shield of faith endows him with almighty power because faith requisitions the presence and power of God. The fiery darts of evil cannot penetrate the shield to reach the vitals of the body. The faithful saints have not even an Achilles heel which Satan can pierce with his poisoned arrows. And the word of God is "sharper than any two-edged sword piercing to the dividing asunder of the soul and the spirit of the joints and marrow, and is a discerner of the thoughts and intents of the heart."

The Bible finds men out. It cuts them to the heart and makes them cry out "Men and brethren, what must we do?" One has seen it so wound and cripple people that they would come and confess the secret sins of their lives to the visiting preacher. But the armor alone is not sufficient. There must be prayer. Prayer that becomes supplication, the most earnest, importunate asking. Prayer at all seasons, that never gives up or slackens its calling. Prayer in the Holy Spirit who knows the deep things of God and knows how to convict and bind the sinner, hand and foot, and bring him to surrender to the crucified and risen Christ. Prayer that is watchful, which expects things to happen as Elijah did when he went to look for the cloud after he had prayed for rain. Prayer that ever perseveres with all supplication for the saints. Prayer that backs up the ministry of the word, asking that preachers may open their mouths and with freedom of speech make known the mystery of the gospel, for which our forbears have been ambassadors in chains of affliction and persecution.

Paul is an old man now in a chain, but he is an ambassador of the highest power. He never lets persecution, indignity, suffering obscure the fact that he represents the King eternal.

In his farewell his great heart is tender. "But that ye also may know the things concerning me, how I am getting on, Tychicus (who bore the epistle to them) will make known all things to you, Tychicus the beloved brother and faithful servant in the Lord whom I have sent to you for this very thing, in order that ye may know the things concerning us and that he may comfort your hearts. Peace to the brethren and love with faith from God the Father and from the Lord Jesus Christ. Grace be with all those who love our Lord Jesus Christ with unfailing, incorruptible love." As he began the letter, so he closes with wishing grace and peace for all who love our Lord Jesus Christ in sincerity.

XIII

GRACE MINISTERED BY THE HOLY SPIRIT

*Ephesians 1:13 & 14; 1:17; 2:18; 2:22; 3:5, 16;
4:3, 4; 4:30; 5:18; 6:18.*

One has read a number of good books on The Holy Spirit. They have been both instructive and edifying. Also numerous articles in papers and magazines, and books which in their teaching magnify the Spirit have been read with interest and profit. But in due appreciation of these sources one may say that he doubts whether anybody has written, or can write, about the Holy Spirit just as we should like for the subject to be treated. One is reminded of the great preacher J. B. Jeter who said: "Well, I must get ready to preach but I can't preach, and I *never heard anybody who could preach.*" Jeter could preach so that hearers were convulsed with emotion, transported with joy, and whole congregations were sobbing and confessing their sins. But his ideal for preaching was so high that he felt the task was an impossible one. This writer is not in Jeter's class and hence is the more deeply and desperately conscious of his inability to write about the Holy Spirit. It seems proper however, to try, in the closing chapter of this book on grace to say something concerning Paul's teaching here about the Holy Spirit, however feeble may be the attempt. Paul has much to say about the Spirit in other letters as do other New Testament writers, and Old Testament authors also. Moses got no

further than the second verse of Genesis before he said:
"And the earth was waste and void, and darkness was
upon the face of the deep, and the Spirit of God moved
upon the face of the waters." The Hebrew participle
which is translated "moved" means, literally, "was brooding." It is like the mother instinct which hovers over,
covers with her body, nourishes the young, as a hen
broods over the nest. John Milton, in beauty and great
humility expressed the idea in *Paradise Lost*:

"And chiefly Thou, O Spirit, that dost prefer
Before all temples the upright heart and pure,
Instruct me, for Thou know'st; Thou from the first
Wast present, and with mighty wings outspread,
Dove-like sat'st brooding on the vast abyss,
And mad'st it pregnant; what in me is dark
Illumine, what is low raise and support;
That, to the height of this great argument,
I may assert eternal Providence
And justify the ways of God to men."

If nothing more let us cite the eleven references the
apostle makes to the Spirit in this matchless book on
grace. For the convenience of the reader every reference to the Holy Spirit in Ephesians is listed under the
caption of this chapter.

The eleven references to the Holy Spirit, expressed
in the eleven verses listed, in Ephesians have to do with
the work of the Spirit in the life of the Christian. In
other places things are said concerning the Spirit's work
with the unsaved as well as with the saved. David cried
after his great sin: "Uphold me with Thy free Spirit"
(Psalm 51:12). Jesus quoted Isaiah (61:1) "The Spirit
of the Lord Jehovah is upon me because Jehovah hath
anointed me to preach good tidings unto the meek; he

hath sent me to bind up the broken hearted, to proclaim liberty to the captives and the opening of the prison to them that are bound." "Jesus was led up of the Spirit into the wilderness to be tempted of the devil" (Matt. 4:1). "Jesus returned in the power of the Spirit into Galilee" (Lu. 4:14). "And they were all filled with the Holy Spirit, and began (and kept on speaking) to speak (in orderly discourse) with other tongues as the Spirit gave (kept on giving) them utterance" (Acts 2:4). "The Spirit said unto Philip go near and join thyself to this chariot" (Acts 8:29). "And the Spirit said unto Peter" (Acts 11:12); "Agabus signified by the Spirit" (Ac. 11:28). "They assayed to go into Bithynia, and the Spirit of Jesus suffered them not" (Ac. 16:7). "For the law of the Spirit of life in Christ Jesus made me free from the law of sin and death" (Rom. 8:2). "But if any man hath not the Spirit of Christ he is none of His" (Rom. 8:9). "And He (the Comforter) when He is come will convict the world in respect of sin, and of righteousness, and of judgment" (John 16:8).

These, with many other Scriptures that might be cited, show how constantly the Holy Spirit moves upon the lives of men both good and bad—that is to bring bad men to a knowledge of the truth. But in Ephesians the eleven references to the Spirit all have to do with the life and work of believers.

For convenience we may classify these passages under the two heads—"What the Spirit Does For Us," and "What We May Do For Him, or Through Him."

What The Spirit Does For Us

First. He seals us: "In whom also ye (Gentiles as well as we Jews) having heard the word of the truth, the gospel of your salvation in whom, having also believed, ye were sealed with the Holy Spirit of promise, which is an earnest of our inheritance unto the redemption of God's own possession, unto the praise of His glory" (Eph. 1:13, 14).

Paul specially emphasizes the word Holy. When we deal with the mystic and mighty Spirit of God, or He deals with us, we are to realize that we have to do with infinite and awful holiness and righteousness and truth. We dare not treat Him lightly or falsely, or evasively. He is gentle, reticent, companionable, convincing, but majestic, mighty, marvelous, awe-inspiring in His divine personality.

He is called the Spirit of "the promise." God had said by the mouth of Joel: "I will pour forth of my Spirit upon all flesh." Peter said that Joel's promise came true on Pentecost. The definite promise was also given by the Lord: "Wait for the promise of the Father." They tarried as commanded and received the promise. Likewise, these Gentile believers just the same as the Jews, "who before had hoped in Christ," when they had heard the word of truth and believed on the Lord were sealed by the Holy Spirit.

Now what is this sealing of the Holy Spirit? Paul gives us the answer. "Which (the sealing) is an earnest of our inheritance, unto the redemption of the purchased possession," which means God's own possession. Something has been bought, and part of the price has already been paid. That payment is the attestation, and ratification of the transaction. It stamps ownership on the property. It makes alienation, and violation of the property impossible. It pledges and guarantees that the balance of the whole payment shall be made, that everything is forth coming and certain to be completed and delivered to finish the complete redemption of that which has been purchased. It is stamped with the owner's name, and becomes sacrosanct and immune against rapine and violence of intruders and poachers. If there is anything more humbling and glorious than having God's mark of ownership upon us and His approval and ratifying pleasure of our salvation one does not know what it could be.

When a farm boy, one saw a cattle buyer press a fiery hot branding iron on the flesh of animals and burn the initials of his name on their bodies as the sign of ownership and safeguard against thieves. It caused great pain to the brutes but facilitated their care and safety. A great apostle said: "Henceforth let no man trouble me for I bear in my body the brandmarks of Jesus." The Spirit *may* brand us with pain, or otherwise as it pleaseth Him, but the safety is certain, and the ownership is delightful both to possessed and possessor. "Ye were sealed with the Holy Spirit of promise."

Second. He is the Spirit of wisdom and revelation. Paul is unceasing in his prayers, "That the God of our Lord Jesus Christ, the Father of glory, may give unto you the Spirit of wisdom and revelation in an accurate knowledge of Him, the eyes of your heart being enlightened, to the end that ye may know what is the hope of His calling; what is the riches of the glory of His inheritance in the saints; and what is the exceeding greatness of His power to-usward who believe according to the working of the conquering power of His mighty strength, which He wrought in Christ when He raised him from the dead, and set him at His own right hand in the heavenly places." In this passage we are told the Holy Spirit is the Spirit of wisdom and revelation.

One would put no premium on ignorance, neither would he defy education. But an unlettered man may become under the Spirit's tutelage a man of true wisdom, while a very highly educated man may, without the Spirit's guidance, be a very big fool. "The fool hath said in his heart there is no God." There is a chasm as wide as the poles between learning and wisdom. A highly trained ministerial friend went out to a plain country congregation and spoke on "*Ministerial Education.*" When asked what he thought of the speech an unlettered countryman said: "It was fine, but if you educated that preacher you would ruin him." The minister had talked out of his heart so simply to the folks that the crude countryman did not know that he was educated.

When Dr. John A. Broadus came to preach our college Commencement sermon, a cotton warehouse was secured and put in order to accommodate the crowd. A cultured woman of another denomination came to hear the preacher of wide reputation; and afterward commented: "Well, I declare, I understood every word the great man said." God's ways are not as our ways, and His thoughts not as our thoughts. As high as the heavens are above the earth so are God's thoughts above our thought and His ways above our ways.

The Holy Spirit will give wisdom to the spirits of willing men. That is what Paul prays for in this matchless supplication. He is the Spirit of revelation. We cannot know God in any adequate sense unless the Spirit reveals Him. God is invisible, intangible, inscrutable, incomprehensible to all man's processes of reasoning apart from the Holy Spirit. Paul prays that we may have an "accurate," "correct" knowledge of God; that the Spirit may give us such knowledge.

Paul in First Corinthians (2:6-16) gives a wonderful passage on this subject. "We speak wisdom, however,

among them that are fullgrown (not "perfect" as King
James version); yet a wisdom not of this world, nor of
the rulers of this world who are coming to naught,
but we speak God's wisdom in a mystery, even the
wisdom that hath been hidden, which God foreordained before the world unto our glory; which none
of the rulers of this world hath known, for had they
known it, they would not have crucified the Lord of
glory, but as it is written:

"Things which eye saw not,
    and ear heard not,
And which entered not into the
    heart of man,
Whatsoever things God prepared
    for them that love Him.

But unto us God revealed them through the Spirit; for
the Spirit searcheth all things, yea, the deep things of
God. For who among men (of mankind) knoweth the
things of a man, save the spirit of the man, which is in
him? Even so, (just so) the things of God none knoweth (nobody knows), save the Spirit of God. But we
received, not the spirit of the world, but the spirit which
is from God; that we might know the things that were
freely given to us of God. Which things also we speak,
not in words which man's wisdom teacheth but which
the Spirit teacheth, combining spiritual things with spiritual words. Now the natural men receiveth not the
things of the Spirit of God, for they are foolishness unto
him; and he cannot know them, because they are spiritually judged".

Here just as in Ephesians the apostle tells us of the
things of God which were hidden from the ages but
were revealed unto us through the Spirit.

This passage in Corinthians does not refer to heaven. It is pathetic how Paul is misunderstood in this passage by so many who entirely overlook the next verse—"But unto us God revealed them through the Spirit." He is writing of "the deep things of God," which can be known here and now because the Holy Spirit revealed them to him and to other Christians of his day, and unto us through his Spirit. They are the same things he tells us about the Spirit's revelations here in Ephesians—"The hope of His calling, the riches of the glory of His inheritance in the saints, and the exceeding greatness of His power to-usward who believe." Let Paul say what he wants to say and does say. That application robs believers of the supreme blessing which comes to them in this life through the blessed Holy Spirit, our infallible teacher and guide.

In this same Corinthian passage the writer says: "Who among men knoweth the things of man, save the Spirit of the man which is in him, so likewise the things of God nobody knoweth save the Spirit of God." And we received "the Spirit which is from God that we might know the things that were freely given to us of God." And "freely given" is a verb form of the same root as is "grace". He says that he speaks those things "not in words which man's wisdom teacheth, but which the Spirit teacheth, combining spiritual things with spiritual words." The very vocabulary of Spirit-led people is different from that of others. "The natural man receiveth not the things of the Spirit of God, for they are foolishness unto him and he cannot know them because they are spiritually discerned," or understood. Paul said literally "the soulish man receives not the things of the Spirit of God." One must be spiritual, or born of the Spirit before he can understand the Spirit.

Third. In the Holy Spirit we have, through the cross of Christ free access and fellowship and communion with God. Ephesians two, fourteen to eighteen says: "For He (Christ) is our peace, who made both (Jews and Gentiles) one and broke down the middle wall of partition, having abolished in His flesh the enmity, even the law of commandments contained in ordinances; that He might create in Himself of the two one new man, so making peace; and might reconcile them both in one body unto God through the cross, having slain the enmity thereby; and He came and preached peace to you that were far off, and peace to them that were nigh; for through Him we both (Jews and Gentiles) have our access in one Spirit unto the Father."

The Holy Spirit reveals the cross to our hearts and convicts us of sin to bring us unto Christ, and regenerates us by His gracious power; and reveals to us our incomparable riches in Christ and gives free, joyful access and fellowship with the holy Father that we may know what is the riches of the glory of His inheritance in the saints. He meditates all our mercies, promotes all our peace, felicitates all our fellowship, consummates our communion, intensifies our interest in the Lord, quickens our quailing heart with courage and communicates confidence in the Father's imperishable love.

Fourth. The Holy Spirit prepares a home for Christ in the "inside man." "For this cause I bow my knees before the Father (Ephesians 3:14-17)—that He might give unto you, according to the riches of His glory, to be made strong by conquering power through His Spirit in the inner (inside) man that Christ may dwell (make His home) through faith in your hearts."

The only renewal in salvation, to begin with, must come through faith in Christ and the birth by the Holy

Spirit. The same is true in the renovation of Christian hearts made foul by sin. The Spirit can cleanse the heart and make it a fit place for Christ's home. We read a sign in dining rooms or living rooms: "Christ is the head of this home" and how refreshing and satisfying the sentiment. But let us beware not to accept the placard instead of the "peace of God which passeth all understanding" which comes from Christ's residence in the heart. The Lord is not a sojouring, or fly-by-night visitor on high occasions. He owns the place. He lives there, gives directions, issues instructions, softens the sorrows, and crowns the joys of those who dwell with Him in willing obedience. This would be impossible without the preparation of the heart by the Holy Spirit.

When Christ lives in the inside man we become rooted and grounded in love. A "rooted-in-love" tree will weather the storm, bear its fruit in season, and cast a shade like a rock in a weary land for the foot-sore and heated pilgrim. And the building that is grounded, or founded in love will not fall like a house of cards which quakes and topples on sinking sand. The occupant need not fear when rains descend and the rising flood rages against the walls.

Fifth. The mystery of salvation for all who will accept the Lord is revealed in the Spirit. "Whereby when ye read, ye can perceive my understanding in the mystery of Christ, which in other generations was not made known unto the sons of men, as it hath now been revealed unto His holy apostles and prophets in the Spirit, to wit, that the Gentiles are fellow-heirs, and fellow-members of the body and fellow-partakers of the promise in Christ Jesus through the gospel" (Eph. 3:4-6). Here, "in the Spirit" seems, because of the context, almost to require both "in the Spirit" and "by the Spirit" as the rendering. The preposition "en" (in) is used with "Spirit." This preposition is used to express location in a place or person, or, used with the Instrumental Case, to express means or agency, when it is translated "by", or "with". Here the revelation is made certainly in the Spirit, or in the power and sphere of the Spirit; also it is made by the Spirit for He is the only one who could make it.

Now what is the revelation that He has made of which we are told in this passage? It is something not made known in other generations to the sons of men. It was a mystery hidden in the mind of God who created all things. It is something that now has been uncovered before the eyes and minds of holy apostles and prophets, by the Holy Spirit. It is something that He made known in the fullness of the time. This mystery is the unheard-of, unimagined blessed dispensation, or eternal purpose of God, and the predestined activity of God, by which He made the Gentiles, all nations, fellow-heirs, and fellow-body members and fellow-partakers of the promise in Christ Jesus through the gospel. In other words, the Holy Spirit has made a revelation that ought to set all God's people right on the question of nationalism, race hatred, and bigotry, and tyranny of every kind. What right has anybody to claim an interest in Christ's suffering for his sins if he denies this right to any other human being? If the death of Christ can save anybody, it can save everybody. If it can't save everybody, it can save nobody. Remember that if you would deny the gospel to any human soul, you are opposing the revelation and operation of the Holy Spirit.

Sixth. The Holy Spirit fits the believer and the whole church for the final and eternal habitation of God Himself. The text here is Ephesians (2:21, 22) where the

apostle says: "In whom every building (harmoniously),
fitly framed together is growing into a holy temple in
the Lord, in whom also ye are being builded together
for a habitation of God in the Spirit." It is plain that
either each Christian, or each individual local church
is growing into a holy temple, both in fact, it would
seem. It may refer to a local congregation but in that
case the congregation includes every true believer. "Ye
are all being builded together for a habitation of God in
the Spirit" surely means nothing less than that the whole
body or totality of believers are growing in unity, soli-
darity, and sanctity and are destined to be the eternal
dwelling place of God through His Spirit.

In addition, to these great graces which the Spirit
ministers to us, there are also

Certain Things We Can Do For Him

Seventh. In Chapter four (Vs. 3, 4) we are commanded to keep, guard the unity of the Spirit. The
Holy Spirit is a divine Person, infinitely wise and
all-powerful whose major work for believers is to sanctify them through the truth, and unite them in fellowship and peace so that factions, jealousy, and strife cannot separate and devour them. It is His office work to
give and nurture unity and brotherly love. There can't
be a row in a church if all the members seek the guidance
of the Spirit. We are commanded to guard, or keep, this
unity as an officer would guard a prisoner, or as an army
would keep or guard a city. The unity of the Spirit
is the most essential thing for the peace and progress of
the churches. If we fail there, hearts are broken, churches rent asunder, and the kingdom of God is retarded or
even defeated in its progress.

Eighth. Being a person the Holy Spirit can be

grieved. It is a heartbreak to anyone who wants to do right if he should grieve a friend. To grieve your Mother unnecessarily would seem almost the sum of villainies. But how dare we grieve the Holy Spirit by whom we are sealed unto the day of redemption!

Paul gives the negative injunction (Eph. 4:30) about grieving the Spirit just after he has said: "Let no rotten (sapros in Greek) word proceed out of your mouth" (4:19). The word for "mouth" is singular and the one for "your" is plural—the mouth of all preachers, laymen, women, young and old. "Cleanse yourselves, ye that bear the vessels of Jehovah" is peculiarly for us who minister in holy things, but all Christians must heed the same principle.

The Spirit is grieved and His work hindered by filthy desires and communications.

Ninth. In Ephesians five eighteen we are commanded to be "filled with the Spirit." If that were not possible it would not have been commanded. It can be done by watchfulness, study of the word, prayer, and submission to God's will in Christ. It is a fatal mistake for believers to think that because they are Christians they have all the power of the Spirit they may and should have.

His power is to be sought and welcomed. To be sure He does not forsake any believer, but He is working in many lives which He does not wholly control. One heard a minister, in a special sermon before an association, almost violently condemn Christians who pray for the fullness of the Spirit in their hearts. He was not any too gracious when reminded of our Lord's promise (Luke 11:13) where Jesus promises the Spirit to them that ask Him. Being filled with the Spirit will result in "speaking unto yourselves in psalms, and hymns and spiritual songs, singing and making melody (psaltering, playing on the psalter is the Greek word) in your heart to the Lord, giving thanks always for all things in the name of our Lord Jesus Christ to our God and Father, submitting yourselves to one another in the fear of Christ." Joy in the Scriptures, delights in hymnody, blessings of spiritual music, thanksgiving, and humble behavior toward one another are inevitable fruits of the Spirit filled life.

Tenth. The Spirit uses a sword. Take "the sword of the Spirit which is the word of God" (Chap. 6:12), says Paul. The sword is a fighting instrument. The word in Greek means a large knife for killing animals and cutting up flesh. Then a small sword as distinguished from the large sword. It was an instrument for fighting at close quarters, which could be used with a quick, dagger-like thrust.

The term used for "word" refers to something spoken by a living voice. It is not the "Logos" referring to Christ, but the word of God which we are to preach in the power of the Holy Spirit sent down from heaven. The author of Hebrews says that it is "living and powerful, and sharper than any two-edged sword, piercing to the dividing asunder of the soul and spirit and the joints and marrow; and is a discerner of the thoughts and intents of the heart." God's word has the power of life and death—"dividing of the soul and spirit." It not only reveals our thoughts but even our secret purpose and intentions. His word is the Christian's message, laymen as well as preachers. It will bring results if preached in the power of the Holy Spirit. God says of His Word: "My Word shall not return unto me void, but shall accomplish that which I please and shall prosper in the thing whereunto I sent it" (Isaiah 55:11). Good appropriate stories may interest people and illustrate the truth, historical backgrounds may increase understanding of the text, poems that are Christ centered may fire the imagination and soften the heart, but nothing is of any value unless the Holy Spirit can and does use it. The Spirit can use that sword to kill and also to make alive. We do not have to beg men to be convicted of sin. The Holy Spirit will do that if we use God's word in the Spirit's power. It is a discouraging thing to read the sermon subjects in city dailies. The piddling, peripheral, platitudinous stuff not to say the inept, vain, and vacuous subjects set forth for gospel themes is distressing. Efforts to pique the curiosity of hearers with sensational topics and misleading word formations seems like distrust of the Holy Spirit's power to use His own appointed sword, the word of God.

Eleventh. Final in the list of things we may do for Him is praying in the Spirit (6:18). "Lord, teach us to pray," was among the greatest things the disciples ever asked of the Master. When they heard Him pray, they knew that they did not know how to pray. Paul knew his inability to pray without the Spirit. "For what we should pray for even as we ought we do not know," he says (Rom. 10:26), but the Spirit Himself (not itself as the King James Version) helpeth our infirmities with unspeakable groanings." The word translated helpeth our infirmities means to "intercede in one's behalf." There is no word for "infirmities" in the text. That is an implication from our conscious weakness and ignorance concerning how to pray. But where there is a docile spirit and contrite heart the Spirit will always hear our supplications before the Father. There is groaning, agony, and pain in the Spirit's intercession. Is not that the best commentary on Christ's awful suffering in the garden which would have brought death had He not been given special strength?

We can't take "praying in the Spirit" too literally. Paul means what he says. We are to be swallowed up, over-whelmed, mastered and motivated by the Spirit. We are to be in Him and He in us so completely that we are one in effort. Our voice will be His voice, His power our power because He is expressing Himself in us and through us. When this happens men will know that God speaks to them. All true prayer is Spirit-in-spired. One read this statement from a man of great spiritual insight. He said that no person has ever been lost for whom true prayer has been offered. His ex-planation was that every true prayer is inspired by the Holy Spirit, and the Spirit would not inspire prayer for anyone who was going to be finally lost. We will not argue the point but would not know how to answer him if we should controvert the statement. The reader's ex-perience is, perhaps, the same as ours; that is, he feels that he has never really prayed until he knows that what he has asked is the mind of the Spirit.

We must take "the helmet of salvation, and the sword of the Spirit, which is the word of God, with all prayer and supplication, praying in every season (or every time) in the Spirit, and watching thereunto with all persever-ance and supplication concerning all the saints; and for me that speech may be given unto me in opening my mouth boldly (with freedom) to make known the mys-tery of the gospel, for which I am an ambassador in a chain, that in it I may speak boldly (with freedom of speech) as I ought to speak." He asks us to pray with asking so urgent that it becomes supplication. He wants us to pray at every season or time, in the Spirit; he asks us to persevere in supplications for all the saints; and to pray for him that he may boldly speak as he ought to speak. This all comes from the unconquerable spirit of a man who prayed in the Spirit and knew therefore that while he was a person in a chain, he was at the same time an ambassador of the truth which cannot be chained.

> "Can you burn a truth in the martyr's fire,
> Or chain a thought in a dungeon dire
> Or stay the soul as it soars away
> In glorious life from its mouldering clay?
> The truth that liveth, the thoughts that go,
> The spirit ascending all answer—No."